D0011357

Entitlement Abolition

How to Lead Your Family From "**Me**" to "**We**"

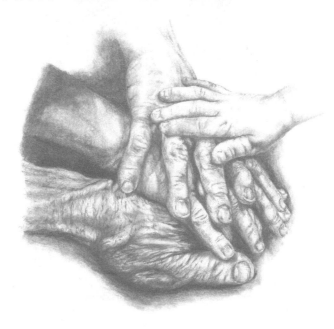

DOUGLAS R. ANDREW
New York Times Best Selling Author

Also by Douglas R. Andrew

BEST SELLERS
Missed Fortune
Missed Fortune 101
The Last Chance Millionaire
Millionaire by Thirty

Learning Curves
Secrets to a Tax-Free Retirement
Baby Boomer Blunders
Create Your Own Economic Stimulus
How to Have LASER Focus

Published 2016
By Live Abundant Publications
Salt Lake City, UT U.S.A.
Printed in U.S.A.
Second Printing, June 2017
Third Printing, October 2017
Fourth Printing, April 2021

ISBN: 978-0-9740087-3-8

© Douglas R. Andrew. All rights reserved.
No part of this work can be copied in whole or part in all forms of media.

www.EntitlementAbolition.com

DISCLAIMER: With any mention of The LASER Fund, max-funded tax-advantaged insurance contracts, or related financial vehicles throughout this book, let it be noted that life insurance policies are not investments and, accordingly, should not be purchased as an investment.

Acknowledgements

An author's work can be unique only in the expression of ideas, which rarely, if ever, claim just one originator. Ideas are the result of countless interactions with people who influence the cultivation of new direction and growth.

I wish to express sincere gratitude for the wonderful people who have helped and inspired me to create *Entitlement Abolition.*

I offer gratitude to Sharee, my wife and companion of forty-two years. Sharee has been by my side rendering assistance and encouragement with every project I've undertaken. She is a wonderful mother to our six children and grandmother to our fourteen (and counting) grandchildren. Thank you for allowing me to name our annual get-away gathering with the grandchildren, "Grandpa's Camp," even though without you by my side we could never pull it off. May we continue to conduct Family Retreats with a Purpose into the sunset of life, with a never-dying passion to add to our book of I Remember When memories and lessons learned.

To my family and friends I offer gratitude for the blessings of life and wonderful support you all give me. My greatest joy comes from being together as we continue to have a Lifetime Learning Commitment (LLC).

I am grateful and express appreciation to Heather Beers, my wonderful friend and editor. I sincerely appreciate your special talents and your encouragement. I extend special thanks to Toni Lock at tmdesigns for her expertise in the layout of this work. And I express thanks to Jolene Farley for her unique and professional artwork and illustrations.

I appreciate the many teachers and mentors in my life. Special thanks to Dan Sullivan, Joe Polish, Robert Cooper, Marshall Thurber, Lee Brower, Richard Rossi, George Pransky, Peter Diamandis, Jim Stovall, and Leo Weidner for your encouragement, inspiration, tools, and advice.

Special thanks to Allen Roberds, Carl Woolston, Emron Andrew, Aaron Andrew, and Bud Heaton who have been so instrumental in the development of our Entitlement Abolition Kit, learning modules, and Legacy Coach program. And thank you to the awesome team of people we have at Live Abundant who work with us in our professional and philanthropic endeavors. TEAM truly means **T**ogether **E**veryone **A**chieves **M**ore. Together we are better—and we can turn this world right-side up!

Introduction

Two affluent guys died and went to the pearly gates. One turned to the other and asked, "How much did you leave behind?" The other one exclaimed, "All of it!"

Another guy thought he had it figured out. He told his wife on his deathbed, "Hey honey, I want you to take all of my material possessions—my stocks, bonds, deeds, titles, articles of incorporation, gold, silver, and jewelry—and stack it up in the attic; because I'm going to pick all that stuff up on the way through." So, his wife did exactly as instructed. Sure enough, he died shortly thereafter, and she couldn't wait to go check it out to see if he succeeded. As she opened the attic door, lo and behold all of his worldly possessions were still sitting there, just as she had arranged. She muttered to herself, "I *knew* I should have arranged all of *his* things in the basement!" (I guess he was going the wrong direction.)

The joke is funny, but true. You simply don't take it with you at the end of the day—there are no luggage racks on hearses!

Many people have devoted their entire lifetimes accumulating financial wealth. I've noticed that a lot of people spend a lot of their health accumulating their wealth, and then later in life they end up spending all their wealth trying to regain their health. Sometimes, people accumulate their wealth at the expense of relationships with their spouse, their children, or a Higher Power. But what was all that for? Sort of stupid, right? We need to touch all of the critical bases during daily living.

TOUCH ALL THE BASES

Just like baseball, we have home plate, first, second, and third bases. Our most important—or "home plate"—possessions are our foundational assets: our family, health, values, talents, heritage, spirituality, future, etc.

We also have another base comprised of our intellectual assets. Wisdom is a product of knowledge multiplied by experiences—and not just the good ones! I've learned more from my bad experiences in life. Other intellectual assets would include our formal education, reputation, systems, methods, traditions, alliances, skills, etc.

Next, would be our financial asset "base," comprised of all of our material possessions—the "things" of life.

The final base consists of our civic or social assets, which we contribute back to society. Most governmental systems in the world have a method whereby we must give back to society, and that normally comes in the form of taxes. But there are ways that we can maintain choice and control by redirecting otherwise payable taxes, taking ownership, and becoming self-sufficient rather than relying on government to take care of us. We can contribute our money, time, talents and other resources to many charitable causes. The point is: it's imperative that we touch all of the bases in life to stay balanced.

On September 23, 1908, in a game against the eventual World Series Champion Chicago Cubs, Fred Merkle, a nineteen-year-old rookie of the New York Giants (yes, the name of a baseball team *was* the New York Giants at that time) was on first base, and Moose McCormick was on third base.

There were two outs, and it was the bottom of the ninth inning with the score tied 1-1. The next batter, Al Bridwell, drilled an apparent single into center field. McCormick ran home from third, and the game appeared to be over, a 2–1 Giants victory. Giants fans poured out of the stands and mobbed the field. Merkle, advancing from first base, saw the fans swarming onto the playing field. He turned back to the dugout to join the celebration with his teammates without ever touching second. The Cubs' second baseman, Johnny Evers, noticed this, retrieved the ball, tagged second, and appealed to the umpire, who called Merkle out, nullifying McCormick's run.

The Giants and Cubs would finish tied atop the National League standings, and a one-game playoff was played to decide which team would win the Pennant. The Cubs would win this game, eliminating the Giants. Had the Giants won that September 23 game, the one-game playoff would have been unnecessary, and the Giants may have won the same 1908 World Series that the Cubs proceeded to win.

The importance of touching all the bases was also shown at the start of the 1974 baseball season. Hank Aaron was a player with the Atlanta Braves. He was seeking the record for hitting the most home runs. Aaron needed just one home run to tie the record held by Babe Ruth, the greatest hitter in baseball history. Aaron got that home run the very first time he had a chance to hit the ball. He sent the ball over the wall. That gave him 714 home runs—the same as Babe Ruth.

After that day, baseball fans held their breath every time it was Hank Aaron's turn to hit. When would he hit home run number 715? The wait wasn't long. In the second week of the season, Aaron again hit the ball over the wall. He had beaten Babe Ruth's record. But first, he had to run around the four bases. The other players on his team watched carefully to make sure he touched each one. If he did not, the home run would not have counted. There would have been no new record.

To make sure your "home runs" will count in life, remember to touch all of the bases— but don't stop with just the foundational, intellectual and financial bases. You'll just score a triple if you don't pay it forward by contributing of your means to others and come back to "home" to make it all count.

Hence, the reason I have written this book is to help you touch all of the bases, to make sure you don't lose out when maybe you thought you were hitting home runs with just your money. This book is also about eliminating the entitlement mentality among children who may have been "born on third base" and grew up thinking they hit a "triple."

BUYING HAPPINESS?

I have met many multi-millionaires—people who have created tremendous amounts of financial wealth—and yet many of them are not happy. They are actually bankrupt in other areas in their lives.

My wife and I volunteer to mentor youth at detention centers, boys' and girls' group homes, and crisis residential centers to help young people learn responsibility and accountability and envision a brighter future. These youth are in physical captivity. But many multi-millionaires are experiencing another kind of captivity—that which their financial wealth has caused.

In a nutshell, my perception is that many people think that happiness or peace will come with the accumulation of things. You can often recognize these people because they're always talking about their things. And it doesn't matter how many things they acquire—they don't ever seem to be satisfied.

Other people try to feel better or happy about life by "worshipping" other people. Younger people may do this through rock stars, athletes, movie stars, gang leaders, etc. Often they get confused when their heroes make bad choices or slip and fall. Many adults do the same thing; they latch onto some radio or TV personality, sports commentator, politician, or business leader, and their feeling of happiness (or misery) seems to be dictated by what these people say or do.

Still other people are "thought worshippers." Trends of thought usually are expressed in clichés that people latch onto. I snicker when I hear people quip, "Now, if it sounds too good to be true, it probably isn't true!" In reality, many things in my life at first sounded too good to be true, and they actually ended up being true! I often ask audiences when I speak, "If what you always thought to be true, turned out not to be true, when would you want to know?" Sooner than later, right? Well let's flip the question: "If what you always thought *not* to be true, ended up *being* true, when would you want to know?" You can't be aware of something you're not aware of!

This happens to be true regarding people's stewardship responsibility to not just their financial wealth, but also to the Three Dimensions of Authentic Wealth: Foundational, Intellectual and Financial, which I'll describe in detail in this book. If we don't capture and leave behind "how to fish" to our children and grandchildren, we will in essence be just "dumping" fish in their lap and actually enabling them with an entitlement mentality.

It's like when you throw a rock in a still pond, the ripple in the water extends to ever-widening circles of influence. No man is an island. What we choose to do in our lives can affect countless generations for the better or worse.

BECOMING THRIVERS

There are five stages of wealth that could be illustrated in a bell curve:

1) **Strivers** – People striving to learn true principles but not sure how to apply them to achieve an abundant life

2) **Arrivers** – People who are finally arriving at financial independence by applying principles of conserving rather than consuming, living on less than they earn

3) **Thrivers** – People who learn how to repeat the process of wealth creation, and thus their money begins to earn more than they do—they create multiple streams of income

4) **Survivors** – People who stop doing what made their family successful; they just want to coast; they stop creating value and hunker down hoping not to outlive their money

5) **Divers** – People who have adopted an entitlement mentality and a scarcity mindset; they live out of fear and despair as their financial wealth dissipates and disappears

Obviously the goal for you and your posterity is to get into that Thriver zone—and stay there, for generations. But it's not something that happens by chance. It takes focus, discipline, and commitment. It takes applying true principles, over and over again, and teaching your children and grandchildren to do the same.

This book does not have a religious or political agenda. It simply contains true principles. But a truth is just a belief until you experience it—then it becomes a truth to you. Everything described in this book I have experienced, and I continue to do so. But it's up to you to discern if the principles herein are truth to you. If they are, you have a decision to make: You can apply the principle in your life to have more abundance; you can choose to ignore the principle; or you can put it on the back burner for later.

When you hear a principle and then discern that it is true, I'd recommend you immediately begin to adopt the truth, rather than make up excuses on why you cannot. Start by paying meticulous attention to the strategies and concepts, then look for the tools presented to best implement the principle. You see many people get inspired (say, to lose weight)—and they may even get motivated (by joining a gym or health club)—but the key is in the implementation. That's why the gyms are packed in January after the holiday overindulgence has put on a few extra pounds. But by February you can hear your own echo in the gym—it's a ghost town.

Different isn't always better, but better is always different. If you keep doing what you've always done, you're going to keep getting what you've always gotten. People try over and over to pull off a transformation (financially, physically, spiritually or mentally) in their lives. But as soon as they experience a little bit of pain or discomfort, they go back to their old ways, and the change never comes to fruition.

NO MORE DUMPING THE FISH

In this book, you'll hear me refer to the old adage, "Give a man a fish, and you feed him for a day. Teach a man to fish, and you feed him for a lifetime." I have long argued that too often, well-intended parents—particularly those of financial means—tend to "dump" the fish in their children's laps, rather than teaching them how to fish. They do so hoping to help their children, but they often end up stunting them.

This isn't a new concept—in the late 19th century, novelist Anne Isabella Thackeray Ritchie, in her book, *Mrs. Dymond,* wrote, "...if you give a man a fish he is hungry again in an hour. If you teach him to catch a fish you do him a good turn. But these very elementary principles are apt to clash with the leisure of the cultivated classes."

Going even farther back, as I'll discuss in this book, The Bible's Parable of the Talents addresses the importance of taking personal responsibility to make the most of what one is given. And in his seminal book, *The Ultimate Gift,* Jim Stovall weaves a tale that illustrates the destruction that can be caused by dumping wealth in children's laps, and the transformation that can come from requiring heirs to put some of their own "skin in the game."

I'll never forget when I first read Jim's book—I devoured it in two hours, then handed it to my wife, who did the same. The next weekend was Thanksgiving, and all six of our children couldn't put the book down. While these were principles we had been teaching our children for some time, the power of a book to reinforce these messages was impressive. I went on to give copies of *The Ultimate Gift* away to friends, family, and eventually to thousands of financial services professionals nationwide who attended the Missed Fortune training series I was leading.

With the first-world entitlement that is rampant today, these principles are more timely now than ever. They're at the heart of what you'll be experiencing in this book, along with a roadmap to take all that you've learned, all that you've gained, and pass it on to the people you care about in a way that can have a profound, lasting impact.

IN THIS BOOK ...

This book will:

1) Teach you tried and proven principles

2) Explain strategies and concepts to apply those principles

3) Provide you with several tools to assure you can implement the transformation in your life and the lives of those you care about

You will learn about four distinct, tried and proven methods to achieve more abundance in your life and for those you care about.

You will also learn how to focus on:

- Responsibility and accountability rather than entitlement
- Empowering rather than enabling your family
- Abundance mindsets rather than scarcity mindsets
- Being we-centric rather than me-centric
- Producing rather than consuming
- Independence rather than dependence
- "Skin in the game" rather than "something for nothing"
- Thriving rather than Striving
- Self-reliant rather than government-reliant

Can you tell I'm passionate about this topic? Absolutely! I'm convinced that if we can get to the roots of society—by nourishing individuals and families with these principles—we can change America, and in turn we can change the world!

Table of Contents

The Entitlement Trap

chapter 1
Did We REALLY Raise
Them to Be Like That?!

*" The worst thing you can do for those you love
is the things they could do for themselves."*

Abraham Lincoln

I'll never forget the moment. I was meeting with clients—a couple we had been working with for a few years—and we were assessing the progress on their retirement plans. We had built a relationship, and as always happens with clients, I had grown to care about them, their hopes for the future, and their family.

A few years earlier, they had initiated a strategy that they had planned on funding with $500,000 over the course of a few years. They had started off right, putting in over $100,000 early on, but had stalled out there.

As we looked at the funding deficit, they explained their adult children had run into trouble. One child had gotten divorced and wanted financial support. Another had seen the assistance going toward the divorced sibling and asked for money to help with a business invest-ment. Still another had demanded equal help, and before long, the nearly $400,000 this couple had earmarked to finish funding their ac-count had disappeared. Spent by their children. Nothing else was left. As in nada. Zilch.

As they looked ahead to the years when they would need the money the most, they realized the handouts they'd given their children might just put them in a position to be forced to ask for a handout them-selves down the road. Instead of self-sufficiency, they were facing the threat of dependency. Their golden years were already looking like they might tarnish to a dull brass, and they were scared.

Another couple I worked with had defined a comprehensive approach to retirement, with strategies in place to pass along their wealth to their children when they passed away. They had built a successful business—a restaurant—that had grown in value and clientele over the years. While the couple was approaching retirement, one of their sons came to them with a request: "What if I inherit the family restau-rant now? I can take it over, grow the business, and that will count as my total inheritance. When you pass away, the rest of your wealth can be distributed to my brothers and sisters." The family discussed the proposal and agreed. Everything should have been well and good from there, right? Well, not so much.

By the time the parents passed away, the restaurant had done any-thing but grow. In fact, it was nearly run into the ground. The son, having depleted the restaurant's value, now demanded *another* piece of the inheritance pie. The siblings pushed back, pointing out he had already taken his share with the restaurant. You can imagine the unrest and dissolution that followed, which was exactly the op-posite of what this dear couple would have wanted for their children.

CREATING BRATs?

During my over forty years as a financial strategist, I have seen count-less clients work hard to manage and grow their wealth, enjoy a life of abundance, and foster a similar dream of prosperity for their posterity. But that dream can turn to a nightmare when well-meaning parents chronically step in and pick up the slack for their children. This parental overreach can come in many forms:

- Covering for children's mistakes at school, work, etc.

- Protecting children from the uncomfortable consequences of their own poor choices

- Buying children things like expensive cars, clothing and luxuries without involving them in the responsibility to pay for those things

- Paying for children's education without including them in the process (earning scholarships, paying parents back at a low interest rate, etc.)

- Bailing children out of unwise financial decisions/debt

- Giving children something for nothing

It's important for parents to ask themselves why they do what they do. Are they hoping to become heroes ... without realizing it may contribute to their children becoming permanent victims?

While most parents avoid the extreme situation—contributing to children becoming what I call BRATs, or Blamers Running from Accountability and Truth—many families inadvertently develop at least some of these co-dependent tendencies. Entitlement can creep in and infest families, businesses, and even communities.

If you were to ask parents why they step in to save their children, they will undoubtedly say, "Because I love my children!" But I would ask, is love something that should enable our children ... or empower them?

BREAKING THE CHRYSALIS

It's understandable—no parents or grandparents want to see their kids or grandkids suffer. But this reminds me of an experience my wife,

Sharee, and I had with our grandchildren. For six days every summer, Sharee and I lead Grandpa's Camp, a dedicated time for the grandchildren to join us at our cabin (see Chapter 8 for an in-depth look at how holding your own Grandpa's Camp could impact your family). During the camp, we share conversations, teach important principles, and experience camping and high adventure. The older grandchildren teach the younger ones the principles and skills we've shared, and it's become a highlight of the summer for all of us.

For one of our activities, we gave the children small jars with five caterpillars each. They watched in awe as the caterpillars made their cocoons, then waited with anticipation to see when the caterpillars would emerge as Monarchs.

As the first of the caterpillars started to break through the chrysalis, the grandchildren were eager to help them with the process. Of course it is natural when we see something struggle, we want to help it out of the problem immediately—and we admired that response in our grandchildren. But here's where we had to teach them an important lesson, one that may be counterintuitive. We cautioned them—if you help break the chrysalis for the butterfly, it will die. They resisted the urge, and then we all cheered as the butterflies took flight.

How often do we feel that same urge to help our children break through their chrysalis? It's tough being a parent. But all too often when we rush to relieve the struggle, we may end up facilitating their setbacks. When we swoop in … it can often negate their own opportunity to grow stronger and to take life on … to eventually fly.

We see the same principle play out in commerce and industry. It's why America is struggling. When we bail out companies like General Motors, it can run up billions of dollars of additional national debt. The government is only staving off the inevitable. Instead, companies need to learn how to be more nimble and profitable, or face the natural consequences of mismanagement or market changes.

BEARING FRUIT

If you've ever tended to fruit trees, you'll know that great harvests don't just happen. They take purposeful nurturing and care. I'll admit I'm no arborist, but here are the basics:

- First, you need to pay attention to where you plant your trees—they need at least six hours of unblocked sun a day during the growing season.

- You've got to take care of the soil, mulching and fertilizing it to bring fresh nutrients every season.

- Proper watering is tantamount—and different trees require different amounts of water.

- Pruning is also essential to remove dead wood and make way for more productive fruit the following season. Here, too, different trees require different approaches to pruning; it's best to do your homework so each type of fruit tree can live up to its potential.

- You must also manage insect, pest, and disease control, which takes vigilance.

For anyone who has spent hours in the yard pruning fruit trees, you know it's not necessarily a good time. It's physically awkward, sometimes downright painful, and the tree doesn't look all too happy by the time you're done. But if we don't prune fruit trees, especially when they're just planted or young, they struggle to survive. Cutting the tree back actually stimulates more vigorous growth from the buds. What's more, the natural shape of a tree is not necessarily the best for fruit production. It's important to shape the tree, and maintain a balance between its roots and branches.

Raising children is an awful lot like raising fruit trees. We need to make sure to provide plenty of light—or knowledge, wisdom, and love—on a daily basis. We need to make sure we're adding rich experiences and life lessons so they can grow healthy, satiated roots. And when it comes to pruning and pest control—the tough love sometimes required to help them overcome bad habits, unhealthy relationships, or risky behavior—this may be awkward or even painful, but it's necessary to help them bring their lives to fruition.

THE TOMATO CAGE

A good friend of mine referred to a scriptural analogy (that I also frequently use) of bearing fruit to speak to a group at church recently. His wife spoke before him and told a story about their granddaughter that I think deserves repeating. One spring, their son-in-law announced to his family that they would be planting tomatoes. His little daughter was excited to pick out her own plant at the store and get home to put it in the ground.

As the family was digging, fertilizing and planting, she noticed her dad putting cages around the tomatoes.

"Wait, Dad, I don't want a cage on mine!"

"Well, honey, all the tomatoes need a cage."

"I want mine to be free, Dad!"

"Sweetie, we're putting a cage on it. That's just how they grow best."

But she really, really didn't want a cage. She snuck out at night and pulled the metal framework away from her tomato plant.

When her parents noticed the cage missing the next day, they decided to let this be a life lesson. They didn't say a word.

About a month later, the tomatoes were growing. She was so proud to see that hers was already bushy and tall, unfettered by any cage. Another month passed, and all the plants had quadrupled in size. But her plant, well, it had fallen over. The tomatoes were melding with the dirt, the fruit a mix of cherry red, white spots and decaying brown.

She was crushed. Her dad explained that tomatoes need the support of the cages to grow properly and produce fruit. She never forgot that lesson.

Applied to the topics in this book, the analogy is clear. Without support, without boundaries, sure, our kids might grow—but the growth will likely be out of control. The results will be disappointing, perhaps even disastrous.

It's natural for our kids to push back, to beg for us to "leave the cages off," to let them grow free. But it's the wise parent who realizes boundaries, rules, parameters and guidance are critical for healthy growth.

THAT IT MAY BRING FORTH MORE FRUIT

As a Christian, I often relate this principle to a passage in the Bible. It's one of my favorites, in John 15:1-2, that states, "I am the true vine, and my father is the husbandman. Every branch in me that beareth not fruit he taketh away; and every branch that beareth fruit, he purgeth it, that it may bring forth more fruit."

The setting for this is when Christ is about to be crucified the next day. Judas has already left to betray him, and Jesus is speaking to the eleven remaining disciples. He's telling them essentially God has no use for people who do not bear fruit. (Bearing fruit means we are out in the world, in motion, adding value, helping others.) He then makes it sound like we have two choices:

1) We can refuse to bear fruit (by not being in motion and adding value in the world), and therefore God has no use for us. (We'll be eliminated.)

2) If we bear fruit (if we are in motion, adding value), we're not necessarily "home-free." It's almost a guarantee that we're going to be purged with trials. But this is only to help us grow even more fruit.

God causes rain to fall on the just and unjust. Just because we—or our children or grandchildren—go through trials in life doesn't mean He doesn't love us. In fact, He probably trusts us enough to throw us a curve ball now and then to see how we can handle the challenge, rise above it, and come out victorious.

But I think we often fall into the problem of assuming that if we're doing what's "right," problems won't come our way. This approach can get us into an entitlement trap. College graduates, for example, will often say, "I got my education; now the world owes me a living. Where's my fabulous job, despite the struggling economy?!"

If instead we can help our children and grandchildren get into an abundance versus scarcity mindset, we can help them see they weren't created to be the clam on the bottom of the ocean, waiting for plankton to float by (entitlement). They can learn to be more like the eagle, who leaves the nest and soars for miles to find its livelihood (empowerment).

As we recognize these truths, it can help us avoid the entitlement trap. We can help our posterity have the faith that they are never given a challenge or problem that our Creator is not confident they can overcome. They'll know that life's tough times can help them grow strong and in turn, lift others who are going through similar trials.

So rather than step in and become the rescuer, let's become the supporter. Let's become the arborist in our family's life who helps them bear more fruit.

GOOD NEWS, BAD NEWS

My hope is that as you read this, you're reflecting on your own family and thinking, "Hey, we've done well by our children. They're productive, generous, proactive people who are taking what we've given them and are compounding it exponentially to carry on our family legacy." But if that's not the case; if instead, like thousands of Americans, your posterity is a little more me-centric than we-centric; if they tend to want-want-want instead of produce-give-improve, the good news is it's not too late to turn that tide of entitlement.

The bad news is it isn't necessarily easy. It often takes a lot of work, smart choices, and what I call REAL love (Reinforcing Effective Accountability and Learning) to help children leave the cocoon of entitlement and emerge as the poised, productive adults they were meant to be. But it is doable, and it is worth it.

SKETCHING YOUR FUTURE

There's an exercise I've done with some of my audiences. I'd like you to try it with me now: we're going to draw a kitty.

Now before you protest, thinking, "But I don't have any artistic skills!" let me just say it's simple. Grab a scrap of paper, a pencil, and follow along.

1. Draw a medium circle.

2. Draw a slightly larger circle below.

3. Now add two small triangles to the top of the first circle for the ears.

4. Now add two small circles—and an inverted triangle just below and between those circles—for the eyes and nose. Finish by adding three lines (whiskers) on either side of that inverted triangle.

5. Next, fill in the paws by adding two small circles with three lines for claws in the bottom circle. Add a long curvy oval for the tail.

6. Not bad, right? Now just erase a few lines, and fill in a few more details, like this … and you're done!

This is usually where the audience takes a collective breath, then groans. I chime in, "I know, I know, it seems like a giant leap from the simple sketch to the completed piece, right? But don't fret. You'll be able to get to the final artwork—it just won't be overnight. And it likely won't be without some training or coaching. That's just like building a legacy of abundance. It won't be overnight, but you'll get there. You can learn the skills, build the habits, and eventually, enjoy the results."

In this book, I will share with you the strategies and concepts I have learned over the years—not only as a financial strategist, but also as an abundant living coach and father of six (and grandfather to fourteen and counting). I will also pass along some of the profound principles I have learned from mentors in my own life.

Throughout these chapters, you'll learn:

- The difference between a scarcity and abundance mindset

- The Three Dimensions of Authentic Wealth—especially the two Legacy Dimensions (Foundational and Intellectual)

- How to develop a KASH (Knowledge, Attitudes, Skills and Habits) Blueprint and develop a perpetual Legacy Bank

- How to hold Family Vacations with a Purpose

- How to make deposits and withdrawals from your family's Legacy Bank

- How to rethink your thinking (and help your children do the same)

These principles and strategies can help you and your family achieve better cohesiveness and unity. And they can help establish a lasting plan for your abundance to continue on in perpetuity, blessing countless generations.

chapter 2
Getting on
the Right Cycle

" When we replace a sense of service and gratitude
with a sense of entitlement and expectation, we
quickly see the demise of our relationships, society,
and economy."

Steve Maraboli

If we look at the rise and fall of major civilizations, like the Roman Empire, we can see a pattern that often happens in families today. It begins with a period of significant growth, an era filled with expansion in several areas: skills, wisdom, knowledge, affluence, and ways of living.

This leads to continued increase, with knowledge, influence and power spurring the development of even more knowledge, influence and power. Wealth and abundance abound ... until entitlement creeps in.

Political leaders, privileged segments of society (and even the poor who become accustomed to receiving handouts) lose that humble dedication to growth, learning, and cooperation that brought about the abundance.

It's replaced by a selfish assumption that all the wealth is a given, that it should continue in perpetuity without hard work and planning.

In time, the abundance and resources of the society dwindle, dissipating until the people fight over the last bits of sustenance. The society is left to start from scratch, and often, it never rises to the same level of prominence again.

WHEN MORE THAN ENOUGH BECOMES TOO MUCH

I was on a European tour with a doctor who had succeeded not only in his practice, but also in financial planning. He was wealthy and lived a lavish lifestyle. He owned three airplanes, several exotic cars, and properties in fabulous places. In fact, he told the story of having recently purchased a Ferrari—something he'd always wanted to add to his collection—only to realize he didn't really care to have the showpiece. He sold it within the first month. Clearly he was discovering that "things" don't necessarily bring the satisfaction the world tells us they should.

He provided well for his children, paying for everything throughout their lives, and allowed them full access to the planes, cars and wealth. But he was mystified why they lacked a sense of responsibility and work ethic in their own lives. He had wanted to be a good parent, and thought by providing for them, they would be able to take his abundance, capitalize on it, and catapult the next generation into even more abundance.

He was just coming to experience that sharing the abundance with his children (dumping the fish), without requiring them to put some skin in the game (learning how to fish), was only discouraging growth and encouraging unnecessary consumption.

As we talked, he wanted to know more about the Abundance by Choice event we present throughout the year, so we discussed the values, principles and strategies shared at the retreat, especially our focus on how families should accumulate KASH (Knowledge, Attitudes, Skills and Habits).

Knowledge
Attitudes
Skills
Habits

This doctor thought the ABC event would be helpful for his son, in particular, to attend. But not surprisingly, his son declined the offer. Why would he want to go and listen to some guy talk to him about the principles of abundant living?

The doctor was dismayed at his son's ambivalence. But then ... I worried for the future of his own abundance when, toward the end of the trip, he was talking about buying yet another Ferrari. Often, having more than enough can be too much for people. Like the world's major civilizations who rise and fall, many are at risk of forgetting what got them there, and can tend to put themselves in jeopardy of losing it all.

TAKING THE WRONG TURN

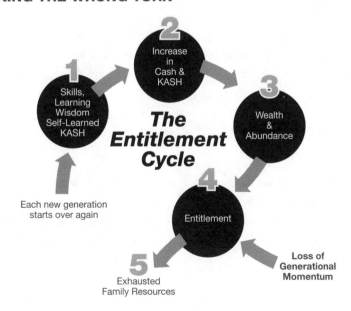

The Entitlement Cycle

1. Skills, Learning Wisdom Self-Learned KASH
2. Increase in Cash & KASH
3. Wealth & Abundance
4. Entitlement
5. Exhausted Family Resources

Each new generation starts over again

Loss of Generational Momentum

This illustration is something the Legacy Coaches I train use in working with families looking to grow and perpetuate their family's Legacy Bank. (A Legacy Bank is essentially a repository for the Legacy Dimensions—Foundational and Intellectual—as well as rules of governance for the financial assets.)

The illustration outlines the Entitlement Cycle, and provides a cautionary look at where things can go wrong. As you can see, families begin accumulating Authentic Wealth by developing KASH. As this grows, it can lead to an increase in more KASH, as well as traditional cash (which is part of the Financial Dimension).

As families continue to practice the things that lead to an increase in foundational, intellectual and financial assets, they begin to thrive. Abundance and wealth become a part of everyday life, and everyone benefits.

But this is where things can take a wrong turn if families aren't vigilant. If children aren't required to practice responsibility, accountability, and financial partnership in things like pursuing education, purchasing cars or homes, or serving humanitarian or religious missions, they can become entitled.

At this point, the family is in danger of eventually exhausting the family resources, much like the family I described in Chapter 1. That couple ended up divvying out $400,000 they had earmarked for funding the financial vehicle they would use during retirement, and eventually their resources were gone. The money was used up, evaporated before it could provide for the parents' retirement, let alone go on to benefit the children in the long-term.

This is where families often lose their generational momentum. They forfeit the cycle of KASH and cash going on to bless future generations. They dwindle in fewer resources and are forced to start the cycle of growth all over again, or worse, live in a scarcity mentality (which I'll explain in Chapter 3).

THE BETTER PATH

The
Abundance Cycle

**Future generations have an
early advantage** and opportunity
to develop KASH & cash

6 — Access to Legacy Bank KASH & Cash

1 — Skills, Learning, Wisdom Self-Learned KASH

2 — Increase in Cash & KASH

3 — Wealth & Abundance

4 — Abundance Mentality Accountability Responsibility

5 — Legacy Bank KASH & Cash (Family Bank)

INCREASE IN MOMENTUM

Let's compare the Entitlement Cycle now to the Abundance Cycle. You'll notice the path is the same through the first three stages:

1. The development of KASH

2. The increase of KASH and cash

3. The prosperity of wealth and abundance

Now, Stage 4 is where things can go right, instead of wrong. When families take proactive measures to reinforce an abundance mentality (more on this in Chapter 3) and instill accountability and responsibility, they are setting up the next generation for success in every aspect of life.

The next stage is where families establish a Legacy Bank, which is a conceptual bank where you can deposit the knowledge, experiences, strategies, and lessons learned by family members (see Chapter 5 for more on Legacy Banks).

Having a functional Legacy Bank in place, with the family actively participating in contributing to and withdrawing from the bank, empowers future generations to have early access to moving forward in developing their own KASH and cash. Unlike the Entitlement Cycle, the next generation doesn't have to start all over again from scratch. They can piggyback on the Authentic Wealth of the previous generation and take it to the next level. If planned and executed well, this Abundance Cycle can go on for generations to come.

Now let me pause and touch on a point that I will come back to time and again throughout this book. Nurturing a Legacy Bank as a family can be powerful, even transformative. But understandably, it may be challenging getting it started, helping family members buy in to the concept, and helping them get in the habit of contributing to it. Children may resist at first. They may feel like there are new parameters being put on them. It might not sound fun. In fact, it might feel a bit like a tomato cage. But remember you can take heart in the truth that parameters, support and guidelines are good, even essential. I have a favorite poem that helps underscore this point, *A Fence or an Ambulance,* by Joseph Malins.

A Fence or an Ambulance

by Joseph Malins (1895)

'Twas a dangerous cliff, as they freely confessed,
though to walk near its crest was so pleasant;
but over its terrible edge there had slipped
a duke and full many a peasant.

So the people said something would have to be done,
but their projects did not at all tally;
some said, 'Put a fence 'round the edge of the cliff,'
some, 'An ambulance down in the valley.'

But the cry for the ambulance carried the day,
for it spread through the neighboring city;
a fence may be useful or not, it is true,
but each heart became full of pity
for those who slipped over the dangerous cliff;

And the dwellers in highway and alley
gave pounds and gave pence, not to put up a fence,
but an ambulance down in the valley.

'For the cliff is all right, if you're careful,' they said,
'and if folks even slip and are dropping,
it isn't the slipping that hurts them so much
as the shock down below when they're stopping.'

So day after day, as these mishaps occurred,
quick forth would those rescuers sally
to pick up the victims who fell off the cliff,
with their ambulance down in the valley.

Then an old sage remarked: 'It's a marvel to me
that people give far more attention
to repairing results than to stopping the cause,
when they'd much better aim at prevention.

Let us stop at its source all this mischief,' cried he,
'come, neighbors and friends, let us rally;
if the cliff we will fence, we might almost dispense
with the ambulance down in the valley.'

Those who prefer an ambulance over a fence will tell you not to worry about the Entitlement Cycle. They say things will just work out. But that often leads to treacherous falls down the cliff-side of life. On the other hand, the Abundance Cycle, like the fence, can protect your children and empower them to lead productive lives.

As you venture into the coming chapters, keep both of these cycles in mind. Watch how they play out in the examples and stories. Reflect on which cycle your family is in now, and what changes you might need to implement to improve. Gather the strategies that will help ensure you and yours don't drop off into loss of generational momentum, but instead keep the Abundance Cycle going for generations of abundance.

chapter 3
Enabling
vs. Empowering

" It has left me with nothing to hope for, with nothing
definite to seek or strive for. Inherited wealth is a real
handicap to happiness."

William K. Vanderbilt, grandson of Cornelius Vanderbilt

" It requires a great deal of boldness and a great deal of
caution to make a great fortune; and when you have
got it, it requires ten times as much wit to keep it."

Nathan Rothschild, son of Mayer Amschel Rothschild

As we examine entitlement, it's clear this isn't just a recent issue in earth's history. You can turn to ancient stories for plenty of references. In the Bible, in Luke 15, for example, the famed parable of the prodigal son reveals how two sons used their inheritance differently. The younger son took his riches, left his family behind, and hit the road to "live it up." The older son, on the other hand, stayed home to continue cultivating the land and family wealth. The younger son eventually depleted his resources so drastically that he was forced to find work feeding pigs. Ashamed and defeated, he eventually made the journey back to his father.

Of course all those familiar with the story will recall how his father showed grace and mercy, welcoming him with joy and celebration. The older son, understandably, was upset at the unfair response for his wayward brother, but the father's reminder was a powerful lesson in abundance. There was more than enough for everyone, and all should benefit.

Now, the prodigal son shows the negative effects of entitlement. But that's not the only way we can lose our children. Luke 15 includes two other parables: that of the lost sheep, and the lost coin.

With the story of the lost sheep, it's the sheep that wanders off. The shepherd leaves the "ninety-and-nine" to look for it, and when he returns, he calls to his neighbors, saying, "Rejoice with me; I have found my lost sheep."

The parable of the lost coin demonstrates how we can lose something precious due to neglect. The woman who had ten silver coins searches endlessly to find the one she lost. She likewise calls her neighbors to rejoice when she finds it.

Any parents who have had children "wander off" from the family fold, or who might have missed out on time with their children (perhaps neglecting them in favor of career or pastimes), know there is indeed much joy in reuniting. Just the same, families who have had children face the negative consequences of entitlement can reverse that trend, establish habits of accountability and abundance, and rejoice in their children "coming home."

Beyond the parables, there are several examples of real-world family governance gone wrong—or right. In the eighteenth and nineteenth centuries, two prominent families demonstrated the difference between entitlement and empowerment. As I share their stories, I'd like to note that I am not endorsing nor criticizing one family over another. I am simply offering their differing approaches as a way to look at how generational wealth can be dissipated or accumulated over time.

VANDERBILT VANISHING ACT

Cornelius Vanderbilt was born in 1794, the son of humble farmers who eked out a living on Staten Island, N.Y. With very little schooling as a boy, he began working alongside his father, who also ferried cargo between Staten Island and Manhattan on a small sailing ship. Cornelius eventually worked as a steamship captain, and in the 1820s went on to start his own business. He became one of the country's largest steamship operators, and by the 1860s he branched into the railroad industry. Nicknamed the Commodore, he was known for being a fierce businessman, unafraid of ruthlessness when he felt the situation required it.

The prestigious Vanderbilt University in Nashville, Tenn., is named after Cornelius. His $1 million gift to found the university was his only major act of philanthropy during his lifetime, and he did it in his seventy-ninth year. By the time he passed away three years later, he was worth more than $100 million—the largest individual fortune in American history up to that time.

He had thirteen children, and was said to have told his son, William "Billy" Henry Vanderbilt, "Any fool can make a fortune; it takes a man of brains to hold onto it." The responsibility for the wealth passed on to Billy, who expanded the family's more than 80% stake in New York Central (a growing national railroad company) and doubled the family fortune to over $200 million. When Billy passed away, the stake was divided between his own two sons, and this third generation is where things started to shift.

As the family interest in New York Central declined, their spending habits went up. Famous in America's Gilded Age for lavish lifestyles, the Vanderbilts were known for their impressive art collection and a repertoire of homes in Newport, R.I., and several mansions on Fifth Avenue in Manhattan.

As the generations continued, so did the spending. By 1972, 120 Vanderbilt families gathered together at a reunion, with very little to show from their inheritance. Most of the New York City homes had been torn down for decades. New York Central, which had once been the nation's second largest railroad with more than 11,000 miles of tracks, had declared bankruptcy, and passenger services were taken over by Amtrak. Today, Cornelius's home in Manhattan is occupied by the retailer Bergdorf Goodman, and Anderson Cooper, CNN anchor and sixth generation Vanderbilt, told radio host Howard Stern, "My mom's made clear to me that there's no trust fund."

You can see how the results play out when wealth is transferred without responsibility or accountability.

ROTHSCHILD REWARDS

The Rothschild family, on the other hand, perpetuated its family wealth for several generations. Mayer Amschel Rothschild was born in Frankfurt, Germany, in 1743. He started his business by dealing in coins and antiques. He began extending credit to customers and dealing in foreign currency trading and government loans, eventually founding a banking dynasty.

He had ten surviving children—five of them sons, who all joined him in the family business. They spread across Europe: Nathan to London; James to Paris; Salomon to Vienna; Carl to Naples; and Amschel, the oldest, stayed in Frankfurt. As their wealth and prominence grew, a French journalist wrote: "There is but one power in Europe and that is Rothschild."

Mayer taught his five sons conservative money management by making investments that produced reasonable profits rather than aggressive returns. They continued their family wealth for generations by establishing the following system:

- They loaned their heirs money or entered into joint ventures.

- The loans had to be repaid to the "family bank."

- The knowledge and experiences those heirs gained had to be shared with other family members.

- Family members gathered at least once a year to reaffirm virtues and intentions, or they couldn't participate in the family bank.

Subsequently, the Rothschilds's wealth compounded and grew as it passed to future generations. While I may not agree with everything the Rothschilds have done or supported, their story provides an example of family management done right.

SCARCITY VS. ABUNDANCE

While things are rarely black and white, there are two very distinct ways of approaching life that can have a significant impact on every aspect of our lives. You can see it play out with the Vanderbilts and the Rothschilds: the difference between a scarcity mindset and an abundance mindset.

Dan Sullivan, the phenomenal Strategic Coach® (and personal friend of mine), has talked at length about scarcity and abundance mind-sets. Scarcity, he says, leads us to believe that our resources, whether they're global energy resources or our own family's food and finances, are finite and in danger of depletion.

When we're in a scarcity mindset, we're in a doomsday fog, without hope of prosperity. We tend to slip into a scarcity spiral, where personal unhappiness and dissatisfaction only compound our sense that everything is limited and soon-to-disappear. We tend to turn inward, produce less, and succumb to a life of mediocrity—if not outright misery.

In a scarcity mindset, it's easy for people to start calling life "unfair." They think, like in kids' sports these days, all the players should get a trophy just for having their name on the roster. They resent the folks who actually go out and practice, hone their skills, win the game … and *then* get the trophy. They want "others" to take care of them, whether that's family or the government. And if life doesn't go their way, if you're happy or successful, that's because you must have taken more than your fair share of the finite amount of happiness and success in the world.

Dan Sullivan wrote an essay called, *The Fairness Doctrine.* He explains that many times people preach fairness, equality, or leveling the playing field, and they usually propose that we need to constantly force redistribution from those who "have" to those who "have not." Historically, it has been proven that successful people, when left to their own goodness, provide most of the jobs and pay the majority of taxes in America. Yet when we get too concerned about redistribution, or excessively taxing those people, it actually works in reverse: jobs are not created. The companies stop innovating and hiring. Why? Because every time they do, they are punished. Disincentivizing productivity leads to continued stagnation in the economy.

In my opinion, we need to avoid relying on governments to take care of us. As Marshall Thurber, the revolutionary attorney, businessman, author and educator (and great friend of mine), puts it: we need to "deal above the line" and avoid shame, blame, and justification. Instead we should take accountability and responsibility for our lives. Government is necessary for some regulations and social services, such as police, schools, and libraries. But when we begin to rely too much on government to take care of us in everything we do, we are treading on dangerous ground.

When we live in the zone of abundance, on the other hand, we want to be accountable and responsible for ourselves. We see the world (and all of us in it) thriving with an infinite bastion of resources, much like the air we breathe. If I were to take an extra breath right now, would you feel slighted? No, because there's more than enough air for us all. If you were to go swimming in the lake right now, should everyone else feel bugged that you'd taken more than your fair share of the water? No, because there's plenty for everyone to take a dip.

When we're in an abundance mindset, we feel increased excitement as we seek new skills, compounding our knowledge as individuals and communities to create and produce even more. We are in a state of "chronic gratitude." In other words, we constantly identify those things we're grateful for. This helps us get out of that victim mentality. If you think about it, the word appreciate means to increase in value. It also means to fully understand the circumstances. As we appreciate what we have—both the good and the bad—our whole life can appreciate in every sense of the word.

The abundance spiral is the complete opposite of the scarcity spiral, beginning with gratitude for what we have. This leads to creativity, as we combine thoughts, strategies, and resources to come up with new solutions and opportunities. We're inspired to collaborate with others and make more of our collective creativity, which leads to even greater results for everyone. We turn outward, produce more, and ascend to a life of excellence and happiness.

SCARCITY VS. ABUNDANCE IN THE REAL WORLD

Looking at the Vanderbilts, you can see how the scarcity mentality wreaked havoc, with the third and subsequent generations eventually exhausting the family's resources. On the other hand, the Rothschilds leveraged their abundance mindset to empower each generation with accountability, and they went on to contribute to and multiply the family wealth.

Going back to the example I used at the beginning of Chapter 1, if you remember there was a couple whose money was earmarked for retirement, but it was drained away in just a few years by demanding children. Here we can see how the parents' abundance mindset—they had been hardworking people who made wise decisions and accumulated enough to set aside for a prosperous retirement—was undermined by their children's scarcity mindset.

It all started with the son who was going through a divorce—he asked for a bailout, without any arrangement to repay his parents. The second son asked for money to open his own bakery. When it started going south, the parents moved several hundred miles from their home to be near their son and work at the bakery. There they were, a retired couple working six days a week to try and salvage a sinking ship. By the time a third child asked for a handout and the bakery went under, they had lost $400,000, given up precious retirement time working long hours at the bakery, and were facing the future with far less than they had planned for.

These adult children wanted to use their parents' money for their own short-term needs, which in the end not only sapped their parents' resources, but also shortchanged their own futures. What if, instead, the parents had continued to fund their account with that $400,000, rather than let it get picked over by the children?

When structured and funded properly, the type of account they were using—my absolute favorite, something we call The LASER (**L**iquid **A**ssets **S**afely **E**arning **R**eturns) Fund, which I'll describe in more detail later—provides liquidity, allowing you to access it for emergencies like helping children. (Liquidity is just one of the many reasons I recommend The LASER Fund as a superior financial vehicle).

The couple could have pulled some money out of their account to assist their children in times of need. But rather than GIVE the money, they could have LOANED it, at a low interest rate. The children could have taken accountability to pay their parents back, which money would then have gone directly back into The LASER Fund account. (On the other hand, the children might not have been so quick to demand money if they knew it was on loan rather than given away!)

The couple would have been able to enjoy an abundant retirement—that $500,000 they had intended to put into their LASER Fund account could have grown to more than $1 million. They could have taken out the equivalent of the average interest earned on the account each year to live on—about $80,000 to $100,000—and it would have been tax-free income! And, here's the kicker, when they eventually passed away, their money would have blossomed and passed on to their beneficiaries income tax-free. Everyone in this family would have benefited, and the abundance would have gone on to bless the next generation.

The truly disheartening part of this story: just recently the husband did pass away, and my office received a call from the son who'd taken the most from his parents—all that time and money in the failed bakery. He was calling to see how much money was left in the account—supposedly out of concern for his mother, but it was hard not to draw the conclusion that, really, he was snooping around to find out how much might be left lying around down the road.

I don't mean to harp on this particular family's experience—the parents' hearts were in the right place, and the children weren't using the money for nefarious activities. But I do share their story as a cautionary tale. Making the harder decisions to empower rather than enable our children may not be our first instinct, but as we incorporate these practices, it can make a profound difference for everyone involved.

ENVY VS. GRATITUDE

I know some families for whom Christmas is anything but a blessed holiday, and it all stems from what lies under the tree—or doesn't. The parents complain that their kids have gotten too focused on the commercial aspect of Christmas, but at the same time, it looks like the contents from the entire Sky Mall catalog get dumped under the boughs every Christmas morning. The size of the bounty isn't often the problem, however, it's the kids' attitude: comparison and competition. After the unwrapping frenzy, the kids will start complaining:

"Mom, why did Suzie get a mountain bike and all I got was just a scooter?!"

"Dad! Sam got a Galaxy phone. Why did I get an iPhone? I hate those!"

"My clothes came from the department store—why did Allie's come from the boutique?!"

Competition and envy are symptoms of the scarcity mentality. It's the idea of: if you have something great, that's bad for me; or if you have success, then I should have the same exact success, too.

The opposites—cooperation and gratitude—are empowering demonstrations of an abundance mentality. They empower people to think, "If you have something great, I am happy for you; or if I can help you succeed, I will be fulfilled."

This scarcity versus abundance dichotomy plays out in society, as well, with things like healthcare. It amuses me that we'll spend hours debating the "right" to healthcare, when the real issue is not about rights; it's about taking responsibility for our health. We all have individual responsibility to take care of ourselves—to be self-reliant. Even if we choose bad habits, poor nutrition or lack of exercise, yes, everyone should have access to healthcare. But we begin to cross a costly line if we insist that the people who choose to be healthy must pay for the people who choose bad habits, and provide them with healthcare rather than teaching preventative measures.

These are the kinds of difficult discussions that cause nothing but irritation and animosity between those who are giving (the tax payers) and those who are constantly receiving (the tax eaters). Just recently in the great country of America, the tide has turned to where there are now more tax eaters than there are tax payers. We must seriously look at reversing the direction we're going, rely on fewer government programs, and look more to the citizens being responsible and accountable. The national debt and spending budget in America are out of control.

Whether it's in our society or in our families, we must do everything we can to cultivate abundance and empowerment over scarcity and entitlement, or we will spiral into lives that are less than fulfilling, or worse, just plain awful.

YOUR GPS ASSESSMENT

Having helped clients manage wealth and create responsible family systems for more than forty years, I have seen time and again the first step in making progress is not so much looking at where you want to go, but taking note of where you are, at this moment.

I illustrate this principle by describing the Global Positioning System, or GPS. If you own a GPS, you'll know it uses triangulation to hone in on three satellites (out of about twenty-four to thirty-two that orbit this Earth for that purpose) to pinpoint your exact location. In fact, it can tell within two square feet where you are standing on the planet. Notice it doesn't care at first where you're going. It wants to know where you are.

Once your GPS has located you, you can program where you want to go, and it will show you all kinds of routes to get there … you can choose from the scenic route, the by-ways, or the freeways. It can also point out where to refuel your car—and yourself—on the way.

As Marshall Thurber once told me, "Doug, you can always tell where somebody's at by where they're at." So simple, but so true.

So I like to make a play on the GPS acronym and use it to stand for Goals, Plans and Systems. As you look at your own GPS coordinates, you might want to ask yourself, "Where is my family, today, on the Entitlement to Abundance Spectrum? Are we headed in the direction of the Vanderbilts, merely hoping that by passing along our wealth and means, our posterity will manage it well? Or are we like the Rothschilds, putting systems and expectations into place to ensure our family will continue to cultivate what we've achieved and pass it on for generations to come?"

ENTITLEMENT VS. ABUNDANCE

Take your GPS assessment to the next level by reviewing the following list, and making a mental note of where you and your family are, today, along the spectrum.

Entitlement *to Abundance* *Spectrum*

Entitlement	Accountable & Responsible
Enabling	Empowering
Scarcity	Abundance
Me-centric	We-centric
Isolated	Collaborative
Consume	Produce
Dependent	Independent
Something for Nothing	Skin in the Game
Striving	Thriving
Government Reliant	Self-Reliant

If the results aren't quite what you were hoping for, don't despair. As I mentioned in Chapter 1, you can begin implementing better practices now that will reap wonderful rewards in the future. But it will take discipline, and it may just take rethinking your thinking.

DIVIDED VS. UNITED?

You can continue your family's financial GPS assessment by specifically looking at your approach to passing along your financial wealth.

One of my colleagues and mentors, Lee Brower, has said, "Traditional estate and financial planning have done more to destroy families and their assets than the federal estate tax could ever do!" Why? It encourages extraordinary consumption. It discourages saving money. And it takes families from a "we" to "me" mentality, with children and grandchildren focused on, "When do I get my share?"

Regardless of its complexity, traditional financial planning, with its emphasis on "equal distribution," has essentially become a process of:

- Divide
- Defer
- Distribute
- Dissipate

When handled this way, wealth is transferred without a system to foster responsibility and accountability. On the other hand, when families are united in the effort to perpetuate the family wealth, amazing things can happen. With our Live Abundant clients, we encourage an entirely different system, one that calls for an "equal opportunity" approach, versus "equal distribution," which translates to:

- Preservation
- Protection
- Perpetuation
- Prosperity

I'll explain more what I mean by equal opportunity and how to implement that with your family in coming chapters. But let me set the foundation for it here by illustrating something I've seen in my study of the scriptures.

In Christianity, we often talk about the importance of "unconditional love," and I agree that we are charged to love one another as Christ has loved us. But often parents will ask, "Doesn't this mean we should treat all our children the same and give them the exact same things?"

I then say, "Wait a minute, if you study the Old Testament and New Testament, God is extremely conditional on how He rewards or blesses His children. We receive blessings predicated on obedience to His laws. There are consequences—both good and bad—for the choices we make." The term "unconditional love" does not exist in ancient scripture, and I think all too often parents get confused because of their personal interpretation of how love is best demonstrated—sometimes it needs to be "tough love."

Sharee and I have six children and fourteen grandchildren. They are all unique—having come with their own factory-installed personalities and abilities. One thing we have learned: if we treated them all exactly the same (at their various stages of maturity), we'd probably be treating most of them wrong. Similarly, when it comes to the family's estate (the resources, knowledge, skills, and money), if you treat everyone the same, you're likely going to be treating them wrong. This is why equal opportunity is better than equal distribution … but more on that later.

You know the phrase, "United we stand; divided we fall"—well, this is a perfect summary of how different approaches can impact your family's prosperity. Throughout this book, you'll gain insights into how you can let go of practices that could divide and dissipate your abundance, and discover how to incorporate strategies that will help preserve your family's abundance in perpetuity.

You'll teach them how to fish, rather than dumping fish in their laps. You'll learn how to create and reinforce the habits of abundance that can lead to ongoing prosperity.

Let me put it another way. If you were going to be playing in a golf tournament and you had the choice of using a professional golfer's swing—or you could use his golf clubs—which would you prefer? I'd choose his swing, not his clubs. Because when you do, you're not only benefiting yourself, but you're also able to teach your children the professional swing, rather than just handing over the pro's clubs.

In the end, we all want nothing more than to bless our family's lives, give them the tools to prosper, and have the confidence they'll continue to pass the bounty along to children, grandchildren, and beyond.

chapter 4
The Wealth
that Really Matters

" What is called genius is the abundance of life and health."

Henry David Thoreau

When you hear the term "assets," what is the first thing that comes to mind? Most people think about their house, cash, stocks, bonds, and other real estate. These are categorized as financial assets, and in the big picture they are really just "things," or material possessions. But I would contend ... wealth is about more than just money.

If you think about it, what are the things we'll reflect on and cherish most when the time comes to pass on from this earthly existence? It's not likely going to be the extra hours we spent at the office. Or the vacation home in the Cayman Islands. Or even the real estate and money we're leaving to our children and grandchildren. It will be the relationships and the memories of time spent with those we care about.

And what will be our greatest legacy to our children and grandchildren? While I'm sure they will appreciate the boost from financial assets they inherit, what will linger even longer will be the insights we shared, the wisdom we endowed, and the life experiences we passed on. Those will help shape the people they go on to be, the lessons they teach their own children, and so on.

AUTHENTIC WEALTH

Throughout my years as a financial strategist, I've seen certain patterns and truths play out time and again in clients' lives. Perhaps one of the biggest truths is that all aspects of our lives are inextricably intertwined, and all have an impact on the level of joy and satisfaction we achieve.

To the degree that we work to cultivate each area, we add to our sense of prosperity. On the other hand, when we overly concentrate on one area and neglect the others, we fall out of balance. While we may be wildly successful in our careers or finances, for example, if our relationships or personal well-being is suffering, we're limiting ourselves (and those around us) on the level of contentment and abundance we can achieve.

This observation—along with insight from several great mentors—has led me to develop a holistic approach to achieving and perpetuating what I call Authentic Wealth. There are Three Dimensions of Authentic Wealth:

- Financial
- Foundational
- Intellectual

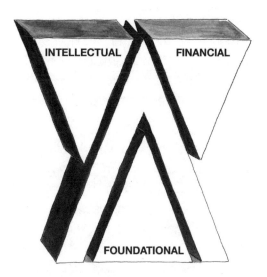

So the question to ask yourself here is: Am I cultivating ALL of my Authentic Wealth? Is my "balance sheet" in or out of balance? Let's take a closer look at each dimension to help you decide.

YOUR FINANCIAL ASSETS – A FINANCIAL DIMENSION

Obviously, your financial assets include anything to do with your money:

- Cash
- Real estate
- Savings, CDs and money market accounts
- Traditional retirement plans
- Non-traditional accounts for retirement
- Maximum-funded insurance contracts

While I won't be delving into these concepts in-depth in this book like I do in others, such as *Missed Fortune 101, The Last Chance Million-aire,* and my upcoming book about The LASER Fund, it is important to explore sound financial strategies to ensure your financial assets are optimized.

Following the crowd may not necessarily be the best thing when it comes to your money, as millions of Americans discovered during what I call the Lost Decade. During America's Great Recession, what Americans *thought* was the best way to save for retirement resulted in the loss of 40% of their IRA and 401(k) account values—twice—between 2000 and 2010.

Compare that to our clients, none of whom lost a single dime of their principals due to market volatility, and many of whom actually doubled or tripled their money during that same time period, through indexing and re-balancing. The secret? It's not just in the commodity. It's also in the strategy. It's in using wealth strategies (the proper swing) and financial vehicles (the right clubs) that provide the most liquidity, safety, rate of return, and tax advantages as possible.

Whatever your chosen strategies, it is vital to do everything you can to make the most of your financial assets so you can avoid the ravages of inflation, market volatility, and rising taxes.

YOUR FOUNDATIONAL ASSETS – A LEGACY DIMENSION

When we talk about how you invest in the relationships and values in life, we're talking about your foundational assets. These include:

- Family
- Friends
- Associates
- Health
- Well-being
- Spirituality
- Talents
- Heritage
- Character
- Charitable giving

For a truly full life, you must view your foundational assets as absolutely essential as the other dimensions of wealth. These can often require just as much attention—if not more—than financial assets.

As we've explored in previous chapters, we can't just take for granted that our children will be empowered to lead full, productive lives. Our society is seductive in its power to sway us toward attitudes of entitlement or scarcity. We must proactively set goals and put plans in place to nurture our individual and family's foundational assets.

There are several practical ways to do this—many of which I'll share later this book. They are strategies that have worked for my family, and they are principles my team and I have implemented with thousands of people through our Abundance by Choice events and Entitlement Abolition Kit.

YOUR INTELLECTUAL ASSETS – A LEGACY DIMENSION

The final category of assets includes the wisdom you've gained through life: your intellectual assets.

Knowledge is what we gain in school and our studies. As we apply this knowledge, we gain practical experience. Thus, the formula follows: KNOWLEDGE x EXPERIENCES = WISDOM.

Do you learn from just good experiences? Absolutely not. Bad experiences can provide "defining moments" that when seized, create tremendous learning opportunities. In fact, one of the secrets to an abundant life is taking your negative experiences and transforming them into positive outcomes. I've developed a tool called The Better Life Circle, described in Chapter 8, which can help you capture the lessons from your setbacks.

Other intellectual assets include:

- Systems
- Methods
- Traditions
- Alliances
- Ideas
- Skills

Your intellectual assets, likewise, are imperative to pass along to your posterity. Using strategies like Family Retreats with a Purpose and establishing rules of governance for your KASH (which I'll explain in the next chapter), can help you do just that.

WHAT'S YOUR ABUNDANT LIVING INDEX SCORE?

As I mentioned in Chapter 3, just like with a GPS system, it's important to assess where you are before you can make progress in any area of life. One of the tools we use at our Abundance by Choice events and in our Entitlement Abolition Kit is the Abundant Living Assessment. It enables you to get an accurate read on where you are, right now, with your progress in all Three Dimensions of Authentic Wealth, and where you can make improvements.

I invite you to take the assessment now—either on your own or with your spouse—to see where you fall. This gauge can help guide your learning as you continue through the principles in this book.

You can fill out the assessment below, or if you prefer the convenience of an online version, you can access it, complete it, and share it online. *(Find it at no cost to you by going to to www.EntitlementAbolition.com/ Resources)*

THE ABUNDANT LIVING ASSESSMENT

Rank yourself on a scale of 1 – 10 on each value statement in three categories, with 1 being "strongly disagree" and 10 being "strongly agree." If it's easier, think of quantifying where you're at as a percentage. For example: 1 = 10% accomplished; 5 = 50%; and 10 = 100%. (In other words, a "10" would mean that the statement is perfectly true in your life.)

FOUNDATIONAL DIMENSION		
VALUE STATEMENT	**Circle your answer** (1 = strongly disagree ... 10 = strongly agree)	**Enter your answer**
We have a clear understanding of the values that are meaningful to us, and we live accordingly and teach them to our loved ones.	1 2 3 4 5 6 7 8 9 10	
We have identified the talents and Unique Ability® that we have been gifted, and we cultivate and multiply them for the benefit of others.	1 2 3 4 5 6 7 8 9 10	
We have meaningful relationships with our loved ones, and we express and demonstrate appreciation for them.	1 2 3 4 5 6 7 8 9 10	
We have an attitude of gratitude for everything in life and measure our progress toward a brighter/bigger future from starting points (where we began)—thereby making our gratitude greater than our success.	1 2 3 4 5 6 7 8 9 10	
We are responsible and accountable and teach those we love how to "deal above the line" by being responsible and accountable, rather than dealing in the "zones" of blame, justification, or shame.	1 2 3 4 5 6 7 8 9 10	

We engage in regular exercise routine and incorporate nutritional eating habits while limiting or abstaining from the consumption of habitual, addictive, or harmful substances.	1 2 3 4 5 6 7 8 9 10	
We have a personal and family "clarity statement" that gives us clarity, energy, and passion for a brighter, bigger future.	1 2 3 4 5 6 7 8 9 10	
We have created family traditions that help our family maintain close relationships and cultivate our family values.	1 2 3 4 5 6 7 8 9 10	
We balance our activities and time appropriately as to what relationships and things matter most in our lives.	1 2 3 4 5 6 7 8 9 10	
We have researched our ancestors and appreciate their legacy and how their lives can impact our own and future generations.	1 2 3 4 5 6 7 8 9 10	
We give generously of our time and talents to the charitable causes that are in alignment with our values and vision.	1 2 3 4 5 6 7 8 9 10	
We involve our family and friends in the charitable causes we support—helping the less fortunate—and encourage them to be philanthropic and charitable on their own.	1 2 3 4 5 6 7 8 9 10	
SUBTOTAL **FOUNDATIONAL DIMENSION** (add the number from each answer and enter the subtotal)		

INTELLECTUAL DIMENSION		
VALUE STATEMENT	**Circle your answer** (1 = strongly disagree ... 10 = strongly agree)	**Enter your answer**
We consciously train our minds and bodies to "unconsciously act in harmony with our family values and vision" and teach this principle to our loved ones.	1 2 3 4 5 6 7 8 9 10	
We are possibility thinkers and have an "abundance mindset" that enables us to create and recognize endless opportunities for living a life of abundance.	1 2 3 4 5 6 7 8 9 10	
We share our KASH (Knowledge, Attitudes, Skills and Habits) with our loved ones and the charitable causes we support.	1 2 3 4 5 6 7 8 9 10	
We continually enhance our KASH and set the proper example for our family.	1 2 3 4 5 6 7 8 9 10	
We have a "Lifetime Learning Commitment" (LLC) wherein we invest time, energy and money to gain wisdom and strive to make the learning greater than the experience.	1 2 3 4 5 6 7 8 9 10	
We are proud of the reputation that we have developed and live accordingly.	1 2 3 4 5 6 7 8 9 10	
We have recorded significant experiences and defining moments in our lives for the benefit of family and future generations.	1 2 3 4 5 6 7 8 9 10	
We have interviewed our parents/grandparents and/or other family members to capture and record their experiences, philosophy on life, and the lessons they learned.	1 2 3 4 5 6 7 8 9 10	
We plan and carry out family outings, reunions, retreats, and vacations with a specific purpose.	1 2 3 4 5 6 7 8 9 10	

We have advisors, mentors, and coaches who understand and help us enhance our unique abilities, the values we cherish, and our vision, and we appreciate the assistance they give us.	1 2 3 4 5 6 7 8 9 10	
We understand and realize that we are responsible and accountable for our own happiness and success and look to see the opportunities in every challenge.	1 2 3 4 5 6 7 8 9 10	
We make our confidence greater than our comfort and make our contributions greater than the rewards we receive.	1 2 3 4 5 6 7 8 9 10	
SUBTOTAL INTELLECTUAL DIMENSION (add the number from each answer and enter the subtotal)		

FINANCIAL DIMENSION		
VALUE STATEMENT	Circle your answer (1 = strongly disagree ... 10 = strongly agree)	Enter your answer
We contribute generously and regularly to the charitable causes that are in alignment with our values and vision.	1 2 3 4 5 6 7 8 9 10	
We have advisors, mentors, and/or coaches helping us achieve our vision for financial security—with a lead advisor who is sincerely interested in our success and seeks to understand our values.	1 2 3 4 5 6 7 8 9 10	
We have cash and the necessary basic resources available to support our family for at least six months in the event of an emergency or financial setback.	1 2 3 4 5 6 7 8 9 10	

We feel financially secure with sufficient resources, assets, and/or insurance protection to sustain ourselves and our dependents.	1 2 3 4 5 6 7 8 9 10	
We have a clear and realistic vision of how we will accomplish our financial goals and optimize our assets while adhering to true principles, employing proven strategies and concepts, and using the best tools available.	1 2 3 4 5 6 7 8 9 10	
We have a flexible asset optimization and tax minimization plan in place for ourselves and loved ones to maintain liquid assets safely earning returns (LASER Focus).	1 2 3 4 5 6 7 8 9 10	
We have a system, plan, or trust in place that cultivates and fosters responsibility and accountability for our loved ones, allowing them to grow through equal opportunities while having some "skin in the game."	1 2 3 4 5 6 7 8 9 10	
We have arranged our financial assets in a way to maximize liquidity, safety, and rate of return while minimizing the negative impact of taxes, inflation, market volatility, and economic uncertainty.	1 2 3 4 5 6 7 8 9 10	
We are aware of the tax, legal, and "risk versus return" implications of the strategies we have employed and take primary responsibility for managing our financial assets.	1 2 3 4 5 6 7 8 9 10	
We have implemented a comprehensive estate plan that reflects our family values and vision to optimize assets by preserving and protecting them and empowering our family with a perpetual KASH Blueprint.	1 2 3 4 5 6 7 8 9 10	
Our financial and intellectual assets are protected from those who might seek to take advantage of what we have accumulated through frivolous law suits or unfounded claims.	1 2 3 4 5 6 7 8 9 10	

We have a philosophy and system in place that our loved ones understand, wherein we assist them in developing their own educational and financial opportunities while teaching responsibility and accountability.	1 2 3 4 5 6 7 8 9 10	
BONUS POINTS We always make our purpose greater than our money and our cooperation greater than our status.	1 2 3 4 5 6 7 8 9 10	
SUBTOTAL INTELLECTUAL DIMENSION (add the number from each answer and enter the subtotal)		
TOTAL POINTS		
Foundational Dimension Subtotal		
Intellectual Dimension Subtotal		
Financial Dimension Subtotal		
GRAND TOTAL		

YOUR SCORE

301 – 360 Level 6 - Superior—Keep leading!

241 – 300 Level 5 - Excellent—You're on track!

181 – 240 Level 4 - Good—Great start, keep it up!

121 – 180 Level 3 - Fair—Lots of work left to do!

  61 – 120 Level 2 - It's time to get to work!

    0 –   60 Level 1 - You're better than this—Get in motion and watch the magic happen!

LIVE ABUNDANT & AUTHENTIC WEALTH

Take a look at your Abundant Living Index Score. Is it right where you want it to be ... or do you have room for improvement? My guess is you're in great company if you have room for improvement—we all can do better! And even if your score is low, don't despair. It's all looking up from here! If your score is high, congratulate yourself on great progress so far, and set goals for taking it to the next level.

My work, and whole life, really, is dedicated to helping families improve their abundant living. When I started my career, my work was centered primarily on helping clients achieve greater financial wealth. But over the years, as my relationships with my clients grew, and as my own wisdom and life experiences expanded, my focus has extended to a much more holistic approach.

To my titles of financial strategist, author, national radio show host, and speaker, I've added abundant living coach. That's why my firm is now called Live Abundant, and my staff includes passionate, articulate experts we call Wealth Architects.

Our mission is to help clients grow their assets in all Three Dimensions of Authentic Wealth, because that is what truly leads to living an abundant life. We have developed very specific strategies that help people experience important transformations in every aspect of their lives.

And sure enough, it's what has helped our clients root out scarcity and entitlement mentalities and guide their families toward empowerment and abundance. These are many of the same strategies I'm about to share with you.

So get ready to discover how you can help your family experience its own transformation.

section two
Breaking Free
from the
Entitlement Trap

ABUNDANCE

ENTITLEMENT

chapter 5

The Legacy Bank

> *" All good men and women must take responsibility to create legacies that will take the next generation to a level we could only imagine."*
>
> *Jim Rohn*

Does your family have a trust in place? When I ask audiences this question, about a third of the hands go up in Utah. When I'm in California, about 90% of the hands are raised.

I then break the news, "I can assure you that your family will never read any of it, except the one page, where it says how much they're going to get." Why? Because most trusts are based on equal distribution, as I explained in Chapter 3. Most attorneys and estate planners don't know how to help you create a trust that goes beyond "divide up the pie in equal slices." But that means you're only serving up financial assets in your will.

All those important papers deal with just one thing: divvying up the spoils among your children and grandchildren! That's like dumping the fish in their laps!

Here's the thing, though—the legacy you leave is about so much more than finances. It's about what you believe in, and how you expect your family to live with accountability, responsibility, joy, and abundance. It's about giving your posterity equal opportunity to leverage that Authentic Wealth to improve their lives. It's about passing on the knowledge of how to fish.

Ask yourself a few more GPS questions here:

- How would your children or grandchildren describe your family's culture?

- Do your loved ones have a clear idea of who you are and what you stand for?

- Do they know your stories of overcoming challenges, facing setbacks, or achieving success?

- Could they retell funny or charming anecdotes from your life?

- Do they feel encouraged to contribute their own life experiences to the family history?

- Is there a "place" where these stories, values, and lessons are gathered?

Part of the remedy for the entitlement affliction is found in a holistic antidote. A system, a conceptual Legacy Bank that becomes a virtual exchange place for your family, where everyone from grandparents and parents to children and grandchildren can:

- "Deposit" their KASH (Knowledge, Attitudes, Skills and Habits)

- Make "withdrawals," borrowing from others' experiences to turn long learning curves into "power curves" and build on generational momentum

- Define and refine a family Values & Vision Statement

- Create clear rules of governance for contributing to, borrowing from, repaying, and compounding the family's KASH and cash (now and in future generations)

Establishing your family's Legacy Bank is one of the first and most important strategies for the development and perpetuation of the Legacy Dimensions (Intellectual and Foundational). But how do you get started? Let me walk you through some of the basics in this chapter, and we'll delve into more of the details throughout this section.

DEPOSITS & WITHDRAWALS

Your family's Legacy Bank will be the place where each family member can make deposits, or contribute KASH. This means a place where individual stories, life lessons, and experiences can be gathered, shared, reviewed, and exchanged. Essentially, you'll want to consider how to:

1. Write or record the stories, experiences, knowledge, etc.

2. Share them

3. Make them accessible for others to learn from and utilize down the road

Say, for example, you started your own business. You likely have countless stories of facing challenges, learning from mistakes, and hitting certain milestones. If you were to write down those experiences, or record them on your smart phone and have them transcribed, you would be creating a written history of these experiences that can benefit your family members. Or, if you want to shoot a quick video of yourself sharing the story, that's easily done with just about any smart phone or tablet. (And if your family's anything like mine, the younger generations are so adept at technology, you could hand it off to a child or grandchild to edit the video.)

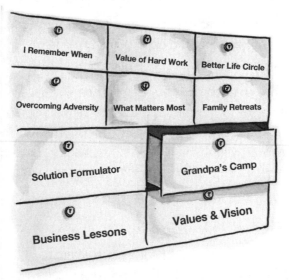

From there, you want to share these stories and experiences. That could take place at an upcoming family dinner. Or you could bring them along to present at an upcoming Family Retreat with a Purpose (which I'll explain more in Chapter 7). Or if everyone is spread out over the miles, you could create an online forum for your family to share deposits, such as a Facebook page, a blog, or family website.

After the initial sharing takes place, it's important to make sure these life lessons are easy for family members to access again and again over time. There are several ways to do this. You could create a library of binders kept on shelves at your home, organized by topic, with an ongoing table of contents, list of contributors, etc., that the family can review when they visit. Or you can print copies for grown children to keep in their homes for their families. Or you could archive them online on your family Facebook page or blog postings.

With deposits going into the Legacy Bank, your family members can then make withdrawals. They can read or watch the stories, glean from others' hard-earned life lessons, and boost their own chances for greater success. They can also feel closer to other family members, getting insight into their life experiences and approaches to life. This way, your Legacy Bank becomes a living, dynamic collection of best practices that elevates the unity and success of your family as a whole!

My sister Glenda, for example, deposits KASH every time she and her husband, Dr. Roy Hammond, travel. In our book, *Learning Curves,* we share how Roy (with whom I co-wrote the book) and Glenda not only travel the world, but how they also make a difference everywhere they go. Through their foundations, Learning Curves Adventure Tours and Smiles for Hope, they raise money for medical and dental supplies, and they host charitable expeditions to third-world countries to deliver the supplies, provide health care, and build hospitals.

Sharee and I have joined Roy and Glenda on several trips, and our lives will be forever changed by those experiences. We always tease Glenda because she's always snapping away on her iPhone, recording the meaningful moments, the historic sites, the important memories. We could be helping patients in the Dominican Republic or at the top of the mountain in Switzerland, and she's got her phone out. Now here's the great part: she posts the experiences on social media, which keeps our entire family in the loop. Her kids eat it up; they respond in real-time and share the moments with her. When she gets back, she saves out the collages she posted onto disks for safekeeping (which makes it easy for Sharee and me, too—we never have to worry about taking pictures!).

One of our Legacy Coaches has shared that his wife captures his family's ongoing memories, life lessons, and experiences on her blog. At the end of every year, she prints the blog posts as a book, which becomes part of their family's Legacy Bank. When their four children someday marry and leave the home, she plans to reprint the books and send them off with a beautiful summary of their lives together.

CLARIFYING VALUES AND VISION

As you formalize your family's Legacy Bank, it's also important to ask yourself: what matters to us? In Chapter 6, we'll take an in-depth look at defining your family's values and vision. But to give you a sneak peek here, you'll want to start by sitting down with your spouse, a notebook and pen, or iPad or laptop, and begin listing the things you want your family to value, experience, and emulate.

You may be thinking, "Well Doug, this list could get long." If so, let it! Don't edit yourself at first. Let it flow. It could include a broad spectrum, such as:

- Reinforcing spirituality or ethics
- Teaching leadership

- Honing communication skills
- Building relationships
- Reinforcing a strong work ethic
- Laughing and having fun
- Sharing in uplifting entertainment, such as plays, musicals, or concerts
- Getting away for outdoor recreation
- Practicing forgiveness
- Learning from mistakes
- Providing community service
- Developing new talents
- Learning new languages
- Completing educational degrees
- Planning for retirement

After you've created an initial list, you can go back through and organize the items by categories. Then you can further organize the categories and items from highest to lowest priority. You can also assess whether these are things you're already practicing, or if they are new habits or skills you want to develop. Read on in Chapter 6 about how to take this list and create a written Values & Vision Statement for your family.

YOUR KASH BLUEPRINT

In the next chapter, we'll also examine how to establish your family's KASH Blueprint. In short, your blueprint will help outline rules of governance for accumulating and managing the Financial Dimension of your family's abundance.

By doing this, you'll get very clear on how your children and grandchildren (and future generations) will have access to financial help with college tuition, medical care, business loans, weddings, and more.

You'll also be able to establish what will be required of family members who want to use these resources—how much they will need to contribute, how they will pay it back, how they can add to the bottom line, etc.

This practice can help your family avoid confusion, tension, and fallout from "that's not fair!" debacles. Just like a building built without a solid blueprint, families can crumble without clear rules of governance. I've seen it far too many times, and the results can be disastrous, all the way from damaged relationships to lawsuits or worse.

In summary, your family's Legacy Bank can become a vital part of your family's ongoing culture. It can help guide, amass, and support your family's growth in all Three Dimensions of Authentic Wealth. And it can help your family thrive on an individual and collective level.

So how about becoming the founder of your own bank? It's an exciting endeavor—one you'll be glad you took on.

chapter 6
United
We Stand

" All for one and one for all."

Alexander Dumas, The Three Musketeers

In Chapter 3, we referred to the concept of united we stand, divided we fall. Now let's take a look at practical ways you can start implementing that unity. And it begins, as always, with a bold look at where you are, followed by a clear vision of where you want to be.

DEALING ABOVE OR BELOW THE LINE?

So it's time for another GPS assessment: does your family tend to deal above or below the line?

As I've shared in some of my other books and articles, true lasting success requires responsibility and accountability.

You may be familiar with Dr. Edwards Deming; he was the total quality management engineer that transformed Japan's manufacturing industries, bringing them to the high level of quality they put out today.

Dr. Deming is known for drawing an imaginary "line," pointing out that many people in the world choose to deal below the line, in three zones:

<u>Responsibility</u>

Accountability

Shame

Justification

Blame

The bottom zone is blame. In this realm, people are always blaming circumstances for their setbacks or failures. It's a victim mentality that ultimately holds people back.

One rung up on the ladder is the zone of justification. So many times you will see people justifying why they can or cannot do something. Justification is no more than making excuses, which again impedes our progress.

In the next zone you find shame. This is where people bar themselves from success because they feel inadequate or undeserving, thinking, "I'm just too stupid. I'm not smart enough. My circumstances, or my upbringing, or my parents didn't teach me that."

Dr. Deming counseled that when you choose to operate in the zone of blame, justification, or shame—it is all an absolute waste of time, energy, money, and resources. It's only when you deal above the line that you progress, and all progress begins by telling the truth. But the hardest people to be honest with? Ourselves.

That honesty, however, enables us to operate above the line, in the zone of responsibility and accountability. Now what does responsibility mean? It means to **respond** with all of your factory-installed, God-given **abilities** to any situation, rather than playing the victim.

HOW $2 CAN CHANGE EVERYTHING

Dr. Deming was a mentor to Marshall Thurber, and he recommended that Thurber institute what we call the $2 Rule with a Fortune 500 company he was advising. Thurber strategically placed jars throughout the company's offices for ninety days. Anytime any employee was dealing below the line, they had to put $2 in a jar. If they didn't recognize it themselves, a co-worker could ask, "Was that dealing below the line?" and if the offender agreed, he or she would add $2 to the jar. At the end of the ninety days, the plan was to donate the collections to a local charity.

Astonishingly, by the end of the ninety days, they had collected over $250,000. And you know what happened to the productivity of that company? It went through the roof! So much that everyone received a raise at the end of the year.

I've used the same $2 Rule with my employees and even with our children and grandchildren on our Family Retreats with a Purpose (which is one of the most powerful ways to instill better family governance—I'll describe this in more detail later in this book). For example, what if we're in Maui and we get ready to get on the boat to go scuba diving, and I ask, "Mindy where's your mask?"

If she were to say, "Well I would have remembered to bring it, but Aaron was bugging me so I forgot," she'd owe $2 in the jar, and we'd have to waste time in going back for it.

If she were to say, "Well, I broke the strap yesterday when we were snorkeling, and it wouldn't have done any good to bring it," we would have said, "No, you needed to be responsible and get a new strap at the dive shop, and that's $2 in the jar!"

If she were to say, "You know me Dad, I'm always forgetting. You have to remind me," she'd be dealing in the zone of shame; she'd owe $2; and we'd have a talk on responsibility.

But if she said, "Oh, I blew it. I'm so sorry everybody. Why don't you all get on the boat, and I'm going to pay the driver to take me back to the dive shop. Tonight, banana splits are on me because you had to wait. I'm so sorry!" Now that is taking responsibility! We all would feel so differently, as she would be making up for the mistake.

You may want to use the $2 Rule to reinforce accountability and responsibility within your own family. Or you may find your own approach. But whatever you do, be sure to help yourself, and everyone else, reap the benefits of these principles and move forward in life.

VALUES AND VISION

So at this point you know where you are, and you know how to use the $2 Rule (or your own approach) for improving any deficits in responsibility and accountability. Now you can get to the next step: defining that vision of where you want to be. They say a goal is only a wish until it's written down … and I would have to agree. I am a firm advocate of writing down everything that is important. From daily gratitude to big-picture goals and aspirations, when we write them down, we're helping our minds process the thoughts, organize them, incorporate them, and put them into play.

William George Jordan wrote a book more than a hundred years ago that resonates to this day. It is one of our family's favorites, as its brief cover-to-cover read contains an enormous amount of transformative strength. *The Majesty of Calmness* looks at how to consciously train the mind and body to unconsciously act in harmony with your values and vision.

It all starts with defining exactly what it is you value, what you want to accomplish, writing it down, and then there's a sort of subconscious magic that sets into motion. Your mind, coupled with your proactive decisions and actions, will actually help bring things about. So again, as you take the time to brainstorm, filter, define, and write down your family's values and vision for the future, you'll be creating a document that will help guide your family's future.

Think about how invaluable our country's Declaration of Independence and Constitution have been. The Declaration of Independence has specified what we strive for—much like a family's Values & Vision Statement. And notice that it's called the Declaration of *In*dependence, rather than Dependence. This underscores the importance of taking ownership for governing one's own life, rather than relying on a "colonial parent" to handle everything.

Similarly, the Constitution has outlined how we will execute our values and vision—much like a family's rules of governance that direct the implementation of the KASH Blueprint. Both documents have helped America protect and maintain one of the world's most impactful democratic republics for over 200 years.

Compare our nation's history to that of countries that govern without the guidance of a sound declaration or constitution. These countries tend to grow in fits and starts; corruption often infiltrates the highest segments of government and society; the people suffer; and leadership often turns over to the next despot, ready to rule without a strong foundation.

Our children can follow a similar trajectory if we don't foster a clear vision for our family values. It's easier for them to be enticed by ephemeral things like entertainment, alcohol, pornography, drugs, or other addictions to fill in the gaps. These "fixes" can lead to a lack of fulfillment, which if not remedied properly, can lead down an even darker road toward the next high, or the next thrill.

Instead, we can combat potential decline and anarchy with a family constitution. With your spouse, take time beforehand to think through what matters most to you. Then involve your children (and grandchildren, if you're already a proud grandparent) in gathering their input as you craft the document. Consider creating a first draft, then take time for everyone to review it, and gather as a family to finalize it.

Here are a few other things to consider when creating your family values and vision:

- What values matter most to you?
- What are your ultimate goals as a family?
- How do you envision the expanding branches of your family interacting/cooperating over the coming years/generations?

Once you have this completed, make sure to keep it somewhere that is visible. Consider framing and hanging it in your family or dining room where the family will see it when they visit. Send a copy to each child so their families can keep it top of mind, as well. And I'd recommend reviewing it all together at least once a year. Talk about how it applies as everyone's lives and experiences change and grow over time. Be open to making any modifications as necessary, with input and sign-off from the rest of the family.

There's no one right way to create a values and vision document. It can be as short as one sentence, or as long as a few pages. It can be in the form of a motto, slogan, affirmation, creed, manifesto, laws, or comprehensive statement. To help you get an idea, here are a few examples:

Example #1: Motto

Together

We're Better!

Example #2: Slogan or Acronym

Together
Everyone
Achieves
More

Example #3: Affirmation

We believe in being honest, true, chaste, and benevolent—in motion and contributing value in the world. We meet challenges with faith and deadlines with hope, and we exercise charity toward all. If there is anything virtuous, lovely, of good report or praiseworthy, we seek after these things.

Example #4: Creed
Our Family Creed

We strive for:

1. **CLARITY**, which blesses us with perpetual *energy*

2. **BALANCE** in the Three Dimensions of Authentic Wealth, which takes the wobble out of our lives and increases the *velocity* in which we achieve our family vision and goals

3. **FOCUS** on what matters most in life, which increases the *accuracy* in achieving our goals

4. **CONFIDENCE** and **FAITH**, which attracts wonderful *opportunities,* that we recognize and seize with gratitude in our hearts

    We *choose* to always be *responsible* and *accountable* for our actions.

Example #5: Abundant Laws
Our Family Laws of Lifetime Growth
(Taken from the book, *Laws of Lifetime Growth*, by Dan Sullivan)

1. We strive to make our future bigger than our past.
2. We make our learning greater than the experience.
3. We make our contributions bigger than our rewards.
4. We make our performance greater than the applause.
5. We make sure our gratitude is greater than our success.
6. We strive to make our enjoyment greater than our effort.
7. We make our cooperation greater than our status.
8. We make our confidence greater than our comfort.
9. We make our purpose greater than the money.
10. We always make our questions bigger than the answers.

Example #6: Manifesto
Our Family Manifesto

1. *We are critical thinkers and problem solvers. We think strategically, transform experiences, and filter opportunities.*

2. *We conquer fear and build never-ending self-confidence and faith. We deal with crises, deadlines, and offenses with faith, hope, and charity.*

3. *We stand for truth and good and are not afraid to defend with pride our values of honesty and integrity.*

4. *We are goal-setters, and we maintain a vision for a brighter, bigger future by focusing on the relationships that matter most in our lives with God, spouse, family, and friends; we care for our well-being in the physical, spiritual, mental, social, and financial zones.*

5. *We manage our time effectively and avoid idleness.*

6. *We are active listeners, effective communicators, and articulate writers.*

7. *We are onboard with an abundance mindset; we are always positive—seeking good, brightening the room when we enter it; we are perceived as a fountain, not a drain, always striving to be on higher ground to be in a position to lift others up.*

8. *We are entrepreneurial, innovative, and self-motivated (with batteries included). We appreciate and understand the four entrepreneurial freedoms: 1) time, 2) money, 3) relationships, and 4) purpose.*

9. *We consciously train our minds and bodies to unconsciously act in harmony with our family values and vision.*

10. *We always maintain an abundance mentality with an attitude of gratitude, rather than a scarcity mentality, which harbors feelings of envy and entitlement.*

11. *We take negative experiences in life and turn them into positive learning experiences and outcomes.*

12. *We are always responsible and accountable—and avoid dealing in the zones of blame, justification, and shame.*

Example #7: Andrew Family Values & Vision Statement

(Note: The following are affirmations derived from the Abundant Living Assessment questions in Chapter 4.)

Foundational Dimension

▲ We have a clear understanding of the values that are meaningful to us; we live accordingly and teach them to our children.

▲ We are grateful for the talents and unique abilities that we have been gifted, and we cultivate and multiply them for the benefit of others.

▲ We have a meaningful relationship with all family members, and we express and demonstrate appreciation for all.

▲ We have an attitude of gratitude for everything in life and measure our progress toward a brighter/bigger future from our starting point (where we began)—thereby making our gratitude greater than our success.

▲ We are responsible and accountable, and we teach those we love how to "deal above the line" by being responsible and accountable, rather than dealing in the zones of blame, justification, and shame.

▲ We engage in regular exercise routines and incorporate nutritional eating habits, while limiting or abstaining from the consumption of habitual, addictive, or harmful substances.

▲ We adhere to our personal and family "clarity statements" to give us clarity, energy, and passion for a brighter, bigger future.

▲ We have family traditions that help our family maintain close relationships and cultivate our family values.

▲ We balance our activities and time appropriately as to what relationships and things matter most in our lives.

▲ We research our ancestors and appreciate their legacy and how their lives can impact our own and future generations.

▲ We give generously of our time and talents to the charitable causes that are in alignment with our values and vision.

▲ We involve our family and friends in the charitable causes we support—helping the less fortunate—and encourage them to be philanthropic and charitable on their own.

Intellectual Dimension

▲ *We consciously train our minds and bodies to "unconsciously act in harmony with our values and vision," and we teach this principle to our loved ones.*

▲ *We are possibility thinkers and have an "abundance mindset" that enables us to create and recognize endless opportunities for living a life of abundance.*

▲ *We share our KASH (Knowledge, Attitudes, Skills and Habits) with our loved ones and the charitable causes we support.*

▲ *We continually enhance our KASH and set the proper example for all family members.*

▲ *We have a "Lifetime Learning Commitment" (LLC), wherein we invest time, energy, and money to gain wisdom, and we strive to make the learning greater than the experience.*

▲ *We are proud of the reputation that we have developed and live accordingly.*

▲ *We record significant experiences and defining moments in our lives for the benefit of family and future generations.*

▲ *We interview parents/grandparents and other family members to capture and record their experiences, philosophy on life, and the lessons they have learned.*

▲ *We plan and carry out family outings, reunions, retreats, and vacations with a specific purpose.*

▲ *We have advisors, mentors, and coaches who understand and help us enhance our unique abilities, as well as the values and vision we cherish, and we appreciate the assistance they give us.*

▲ *We understand and realize that we are responsible and accountable for our own happiness and success, and we look to see the opportunities in every challenge.*

▲ *We make our confidence greater than our comfort, and we make our contributions greater than the rewards we receive.*

Financial Dimension

▲ *We contribute generously and regularly to the charitable causes that are in alignment with our values and vision.*

▲ *We have advisors, mentors, and/or coaches helping us achieve our vision for financial security—with a lead advisor who is sincerely interested in our success and who seeks to understand our values.*

▲ *We have cash and the necessary basic resources available to support our individual families for at least six months in the event of an emergency or financial setback.*

▲ *We feel financially secure with sufficient resources, assets, and/or insurance protection to sustain ourselves and our dependents.*

▲ *We have a clear and realistic vision of how we will accomplish our financial goals and optimize our assets by adhering to true principles, employing proven strategies and concepts, and using the best tools available.*

▲ *We have a flexible asset optimization and tax minimization plan in place for ourselves and our loved ones to maintain Liquid Assets Safely Earning Returns (LASER focus).*

▲ *We have a system, plan, and trust in place that cultivates and fosters responsibility and accountability for our loved ones, allowing them to grow through equal opportunities, while having some "skin in the game."*

▲ *We have arranged our financial assets in a way to maximize liquidity, safety, and rate of return—while minimizing the negative impact of taxes, inflation, market volatility, and economic uncertainty.*

▲ *We are aware of the tax, legal, and "risk versus return" implications of the strategies we have employed and take primary responsibility for managing our financial assets.*

▲ *We have implemented a comprehensive estate plan that reflects our family values and vision to: 1) optimize assets by preserving and protecting them, and 2) to empower our family with a perpetual KASH Blueprint.*

▲ *Our financial and intellectual assets are protected from those who might seek to take advantage of what we have accumulated through frivolous law suits or unfounded claims.*

▲ *We have a philosophy and system in place that our loved ones understand, wherein we assist them in developing their own educational and financial opportunities, while teaching responsibility and accountability.*

STARTING YOUR KASH BLUEPRINT

Throughout the book we've discussed the importance of developing and accumulating KASH (Knowledge, Attitudes, Skills and Habits). One way to ensure that your family's KASH flow stays positive is to put a plan in place—with a KASH Blueprint.

Your blueprint will outline governing principles that can guide your family's strategies with your financial assets. These strategies should apply to every practical financial aspect of life, such as:

- Education
- Health/medical costs
- Emergency needs
- Business ventures/loans
- Personal loans
- Supplemental income
- Weddings
- Personal residence
- Family enrichment, retreats, and vacations with a purpose
- Charitable distributions
- Religious, humanitarian, or charitable missions

In the Entitlement Abolition Kit, we dedicate one of the four modules entirely to a thorough exploration of the KASH Blueprint. This module helps families identify their KASH assets, outline their rules of governance, and put together an overall blueprint for maintaining and even

increasing KASH for generations to come. Like each of the four modules, it is available as a stand-alone guide, or for those interested in all
four pillars of Entitlement Abolition, it is available as part of the comprehensive four-module kit.

To help you get a better idea of how your KASH Blueprint can make a
difference, I'll build on the basics introduced in the previous chapter.

BLUEPRINT ON THE BEACH

My family gathers for regular Family Retreats with a Purpose, where
we reinforce our rules of governance for our KASH Blueprint. Every
two years, we hold ours in Hawaii. Now you might have imagined that
Daddy Doug and Mommy Sharee pay for the entire trip, since we're
established and our kids are grown. But that would only teach entitlement. So instead, we empower our children to be responsible for their
own travel and expenses.

They use strategies like credit card mileage to cover airfare (with cards
they're responsible with), and we've also bought time shares for pen-
nies on the dollar directly from owners who wanted to liquidate them
(or on the resale market). Many times the sellers begged us to simply
bring their delinquent property taxes current, and they would gladly
deed over their time share to us. We often rent out half the time shares,
which pays for maintenance fees on ours. We pool our money and go
grocery shopping and fix many of the meals in the condos. This way
we can meet in Maui almost as inexpensively as at home, and our children maintain their own accountability in joining the vacation.

Now there have been times when one child or another might not have
had the means to pay for all of his or her trip. In those cases, we've
outlined governing principles that allow the child to present a plan for
contributing something of equal value. For example, one child proposed a plan to paint and provide fix-up labor on our family condo in
St. George in exchange for her share of the meal budget in Hawaii.

This not only empowered her to join us in an otherwise financially tough year, but it provided for maintenance needs we had, and it avoided a situation where, if we had just swooped in and paid for her trip without alternative compensation, the other children could have developed a degree of resentment. It was a win-win and satisfied the rules of governance.

BLUEPRINT IN EDUCATION

I often shock audiences when I propose, "You should NOT be paying for your child's college education." I usually hear a few gasps, maybe even boos in the crowd. But when I go on to frame education funding from an empowerment versus entitlement perspective, the audience begins to understand.

When your children take ownership for paying for their college education, things shift. The education is no longer "something they deserve," along with a nice juicy career that "the world owes them" at the end of the degree; it's something they are investing in. They're putting some skin in the game. And the accountability is powerful.

Now am I proposing they take out all kinds of traditional student loans? Not if you have the means to be the bank (or they are motivated to pursue academic, athletic, or leadership scholarships). If you have the resources, then you become the lender, with a low interest rate they can pay over a reasonable amount of time. Your children write up the contract, put the plan in place, and carry it through.

What if they run into tough times and can't pay? Then the contract should have "alternative payment methods" written in, whereby they can provide another means of repayment, such as providing maintenance for your home or second home, or bookkeeping for your business, or something that adds value.

My wife and I both worked our way through college. I worked at Kentucky Fried Chicken, and Sharee worked at a bookstore. I did earn scholarships, as did she. But we worked twenty-five to thirty hours a week while in school and had excellent study habits because we had to budget our time. By comparison, many of our friends got very poor grades because their parents just constantly shelled out the tuition, fees, room, and board.

Hence, Sharee and I, when raising our six children, decided that we would never lead them to believe that we would pay for their college education. We provided equal opportunities. If they got a scholarship or they saved, we would match it, even for a semester abroad. But they had to go abroad with purpose—to study and get As—not just to vacation.

When our daughter Ashley took advantage of our equal opportunity offer to go on one semester abroad, she had such an over-the-top learning experience, she came home and realized that she wanted to have one more.

"Mom, Dad ... I loved Israel and Egypt. There's one more place I'd like to study—New Zealand. It coincides with my minor in recreational development, and I can still take classes toward my accounting major."

"Sounds good Ashley—do you have your Solution Formulator?"

"Oh, I forgot. Let me run up and fill it out really quickly."

Now, the Solution Formulator is one of the many tools we keep in our family tool belt, along with The Opportunity BREAK-Through, The Project Clarifier, The Appreciation Accelerator, and others. These are straight-forward forms that walk you through analyzing future goals or past experiences, help you track the learning and the opportunities, and then assess it all to springboard yourself to a better future. These are more day-to-day tools, and we have others that are used on a monthly or quarterly basis (we call those toolbox tools), and still others that are ideal for annual individual reviews and life planning (toolshed tools). *(Try some of our most popular tools at www.EntitlementAbolition.com/Resources.)*

Well, Ashley grabbed this tool belt tool, and one hour later she bounced back downstairs having "sold" herself on the idea, including a specific target date and action steps to achieve her goal.

"I'm convinced that I need to do this before I graduate—it's an opportunity that will help me learn so much. I've outlined the obstacles, too. But I have a corresponding strategy to overcome each obstacle. Of course, I'll graduate a semester later than originally planned, but it actually works out because now graduation will dovetail with my career path even better. I've already used all my savings on Israel and Egypt, but I do still have my car. I love it, but I can sell it and get at least $2,000 on it. (I'll just save up and buy another car when I get back.) So after I sell the car, I'll still be short $1,500 for New Zealand."

"Okay, what's your plan for that?"

"Well Mom and Dad, if you could loan me $1,500, when I get back I can jump right back into working, and I'll repay you $500 a month for three months."

"Okay, let's see, your plan looks solid, but what if you extended the repayment period to make it more doable? We'd be fine with $300 a month for five months, that way you can save a little extra to buy another car sooner."

The loan was approved; Ashley grew from her incredible learning experiences in New Zealand; and true to her word, she repaid the loan when she returned. Rather than just asking for Mom and Dad's money, she developed the strategy, proposed the solution, and fulfilled the very obligations that *she* designed.

I've found it's critical for children to be heavily involved in thinking through the strategy, devising the approach, and following through. Otherwise, if we as parents say, "I have the answer. I think you should do it this way or that way ..." if something goes awry, they will often come back and blame you. Instead, when they are the architect of their future, the accountability falls on them, for better or for worse, and they naturally own the situation.

Many of our clients have implemented a similar approach to their children's education. Becoming the lender is often easy for them, as they can pull money from the financial vehicle we propose for many of our clients, The LASER Fund. It enables them to fund the education tax-free, and the children's re-payments simply go back into the account to go on and earn additional interest over time.

However you do it, I recommend that you include education in your family's KASH Blueprint. Empower your children and grandchildren to take part in funding their own education by pursuing scholarships or borrowing from you.

BLUEPRINT FOR WHEN YOU'RE GONE

The KASH Blueprint should also include very specific rules of governance for when you're gone. This is where the advisors I train diverge from typical estate planners, who recommend equal distribution. As I explained in Chapter 4, that approach only leads to the "divided we fall" effect, often causing resentment among children or grandchildren, the "what's in it for me" mentality, and eventual dissipation of wealth.

On the other hand, the advisors I endorse help clients develop an Equal Opportunity Trust, which sets the stage for generational wealth. It brings new life and resources to future generations in a way that fosters responsibility and accountability.

With an Equal Opportunity Trust, you have in writing a plan for your children, grandchildren, and future generations to continue carrying out the KASH Blueprint. They will be able to borrow from the family bank for things like education, charitable efforts, personal emergencies, and more. As they repay the bank at low interest rates, the cash continues to fund the KASH in perpetuity. As the money in the bank is placed in smart financial vehicles, such as The LASER Fund contracts, it can continue to grow, as well.

The family bank, of course, is a repository for more than just money. It's also where your family's growing foundational and intellectual assets are gathered and shared, in printed or digital form. It essentially becomes the Fort Knox for all things valuable and abundant in your family.

For our family, Sharee and I have put together an official, written document that encapsulates our rules of governance for situations like taking "loans" from the family bank for education, religious missions, business ventures, etc. The document goes beyond outlining guidelines for just the Financial Dimension, however; it includes our approach for capitalizing on the Foundational and Intellectual Dimensions of Authentic Wealth, as well. We have named it the True Wealth Philosophy for Our Family Legacy Bank, and a template of it is included in The KASH Blueprint Module of the Entitlement Abolition Kit.

Imagine your future generations reaping the rewards of your efforts now, as you turn the tide of entitlement to empowerment and establish your own family bank. The possibilities for growth and strength are endless. Seize this moment, plan now, make the changes you need to establish your rules of governance, and transform your family for great things to come.

chapter 7
Family Retreats
with a Purpose

" I sustain myself with the love of family."

Maya Angelou

We've arrived by Jeep, by plane, by car and by Harley. We've gathered at the family cabin in the Wasatch Mountains, the condo in St. George, the timeshares in Hawaii, and even the family room at our house. It doesn't matter how you get there or where you gather; it just matters that you get together, and that you do so with a purpose.

I'm talking about Family Retreats with a Purpose, an important tool for developing the Legacy Dimensions in your family. Family Retreats with a Purpose can be as simple as an evening at your home or as elaborate as a several-day vacation. It can be held in conjunction with holidays, like Thanksgiving, Christmas, or New Year's. It can also be a one-day getaway to an amusement park or a long weekend at the

Grand Canyon. The idea is to get together regularly (at least once a year, if not more), and along with fun activities, schedule time to reinforce family values, and participate in meaningful exercises.

These "purpose driven adventures" allow everyone to be involved and improve the family communication and unity. I could go on and on about the power of celebrating both the fun and fundamentals of life. It's a chance to slow the pace, create lasting memories, and pass along the values, beliefs, and experiences that matter to us. Essentially, you get away to come together.

For the past several years, Sharee and I have planned these Family Retreats with a Purpose. The concept sprang from professional strategies I've learned in collaborating with some of the top entrepreneurial think tanks in the country. It's been a blessing to associate with achievers on this level—each year I'm overwhelmed at how many true principles I've learned by gathering with some of America's most successful entrepreneurs.

Holding retreats is something we teach at our Abundance by Choice events, and it's also one of the modules in the Entitlement Abolition Kit. This is such a powerful vehicle for family unity and growth, I recommend taking a more in-depth look at how to plan yours. But just to give you an idea, here's how you can get started:

- **Schedule It** – These getaways can be as short as an evening or as long as a week. Find what works for you and your schedule, and put it on everyone's calendar.

- **Where in the World?** – Next, decide where you'll go. We've done Family Retreats with a Purpose at locations in Hawaii and the Wind Rivers of Wyoming, but we've also done retreats that are just an evening at the house or the family cabin. It doesn't have to be expensive or luxurious; the point is just to get away from the day-to-day cares and distractions and focus on time together as a family.

- **Plan Meaningful Activities** – This is more than a regular vacay. To get the most out of your getaway, you'll want to plan purposeful activities. Borrow from our family activities—some of which I describe in my book *Learning Curves* and which I'll illustrate later in this book, such as Unacceptable Detours & Dead Ends, What Matters Most, and I Remember When—or create your own. And don't be surprised if at first you encounter some resistance to the meaningful activities (you likely will), but when your family experiences even one of these sessions, the bonding that follows can make everyone a believer. (Remember, recreate can also mean "re-create" as you sharpen your focus on the important things in life.)

- **Vacate from the "Busy-ness" of Life** – Make your retreat a stress-free zone. Avoid the distractions of work, school, email, social media, etc., by encouraging time away from electronics so you can focus on the family.

- **Load Up on Fun** - These events are not just serious. We've done Retreats with a Purpose that include camping, fishing, hiking, biking, snorkeling, scuba diving, golfing, etc. The secret recipe is to not only make them significant, but also to make them fun!

Now keep in mind, sometimes "family" doesn't necessarily mean father, mother, and children. It can be just you and your spouse (Sharee and I get away for a long weekend at least every quarter at our cabin). You can plan it with your immediate family, or even extended family (of course this also applies to friend getaways, too). And of course you can plan Retreats with a Purpose with your work team.

These intentional retreats, along with specific exercises and activities incorporated, have the power to transform your family or group, just as they have ours. As we've gathered our family together we've taken on topics such as:

- How to teach responsibility and accountability

- How to avoid making serious mistakes during your lifetime

- How to determine what matters most

- How to transform negative experiences in life into positive outcomes

- How to become an intentional family

- How to develop a master plan for your bigger future

To give you an idea of what has worked for the Andrew family, here's the general flow of things at our biannual retreats in Maui, Hawaii, where we gather with the entire family, including adult children and their families:

- We typically get away together for seven to ten days.

- Before going, we determine a few things: primary purpose, secondary purpose, theme, and focused reading (uplifting books—one to read before arriving, one to read while there).

- Once there, we gather every morning for a one-hour devotional.

- The one-hour devotional is broken into two or three segments.

- The first and/or second segments focus on different aspects of the Legacy Dimensions (Intellectual and Foundational), and are taught by different adult family members.

- The third segment is usually a fun activity or game designed to engage the children.

- We play, play, play the rest of the day.

- Then we gather for dinner at night and share I Remember When stories (for more on I Remember When stories, see Chapter 9).

- We follow dinner with an hour-long session, again broken into two or three segments.

- The first segment delves into an aspect of our focused reading book.

- The second segment focuses on family vision and personal goals (all reinforcing our Legacy Bank).

- The third segment is story time and fun for the children.

- In addition, we enact the $2 Rule (explained in Chapter 6) the entire trip—which is a fun way to make sure everyone deals above the line of blame, justification, and shame.

- We also have everyone focus on physical health by trying to cut calorie intake, wearing pedometers, and joining in optional family exercise at 7 am.

Examples of our detailed Family Retreat with a Purpose Agendas are included in Module 3 of the Entitlement Abolition Kit.

MAUI MOJO

To illustrate, our family meets in Maui every two years. Each of our grown children plans ahead, saves, and does what it takes to be able to join us (as I've mentioned, we have used strategies to get time-shares for less). They bring their children, and it's an incredible week of memory making.

While there, we ask our children to take fifteen minutes and write down their response to this question: when we meet here two years from today, looking back, what has to have happened for you to be happy with the progress that you have made with all of your assets?

They go through and record their goals in all Three Dimensions of Authentic Wealth. Then, we have them answer: what are the biggest **B**arriers, roadblocks, and hindrances, that need to be eliminated in order for you to succeed? This increases the likelihood they will achieve that vision from about 55%, up to over 90%.

Then, we have them identify the greatest **R**esources they need to utilize in order to do so, and then identify the best **E**xperiences they can draw from or want to have. Finally, they list the **A**ction steps they are going to take and the **K**nowledge they need to fulfill their goals. This dramatically increases the chances that these things will come to fruition. Hence, the acronym BREAK means you're giving them a "break"—an Opportunity BREAK-Through.

Whenever we have done this, every one of our children has achieved what seemed to be nearly impossible within that two-year time frame, because we all got on board in an abundance mindset support group to help one another.

I remember one year in Maui we were about to go around the family circle with our six children and their spouses to share what has to happen in their lives for them to be happy with the progress they made during the next two years. My son-in-law Scott suggested that we take a moment and share one thing that we wrote down two years earlier and see if it came to fruition. What a great idea!

Talk about an amazing payday as a parent! Going right down the list, our six children and their families reported on one of the top three things that they had circled as most important to them during that time period, and how it was accomplished. That included everything from finding a spouse, to overcoming infertility issues to start a family, to buying a home, to pursuing higher education with the help of a scholarship, and a great new job. And even though they could not see how it would come to fruition two years earlier, it had all happened. This is the power of consciously training the mind and body to unconsciously act in harmony with your values and your vision.

GOING THE EXTRA MILE, LITERALLY

As I mentioned, it's also become a tradition for everyone to wear pedometers throughout our Maui trips. It started as a way to encourage more physical activity and well-being on a trip to Hawaii back in 2005.

That year, everyone who logged 10,000 steps each day received $10 toward dinner from our Legacy Bank. For every 1,000 steps over 10,000, an additional dollar was awarded.

At 5:30 pm each day, we gathered as a family for dinner and disclosed our pedometer results, then reset the meters for the next twenty-four-hour measurement. We kicked off the program in the airport, and it was amazing to see what it inspired. Instead of staying seated, some family members got up and began striding through the concourse until our flight was called. By the end of the week, the competition got to the point that many family members were getting up by 5 am and walking or running over 35,000 steps before breakfast! At mealtime, we also cut calorie intake by sharing appetizers, entrées, and desserts. By the time we came home from this vacation, everyone had lost weight.

In the years since, the pedometer competition has become even more heated, and we've added more cash prizes for total achievement throughout the trip—more than $200 for first place! It's been a fun way for the entire family to take care of their bodies as much as their minds and souls throughout the retreat.

BANKING ON OUR LEGACY

During our Family Retreats with a Purpose, we ask our family members to make deposits in the Legacy Bank, as well as withdrawals. During our morning devotional or evening session, we set aside time for each adult child and spouse to report, verbally and in writing, what they have done since the last family retreat to enhance all Three Dimensions of Authentic Wealth: Intellectual, Foundational, and Financial. We take the written version and add it to our family archive so future generations can learn from (in other words, make withdrawals on) these great accomplishments and life lessons.

For example, at one retreat, our children made a withdrawal on my experience, where I taught how to buy a house with no down payment and without a substantial credit history. As a result, two of our children, who were in their early twenties at the time and had just recently wed, were able to purchase beautiful homes with no money down. At a later retreat, these children then made a deposit of the experience they gained. They explained how they did this and how they each were now building new houses using the same wisdom.

During one of our retreats, we also focused on charitable giving. We took the time to teach everyone about the principle of abundance and the law of the harvest. We taught our children that when you give, the world gives back. We discussed in detail the parable of the talents in the New Testament, book of Matthew, Chapter 25, and the parable of the pounds as found in the book of Luke, Chapter 19.

As parents, we have always emphasized that when much is given, much is required. We invited our children to make a withdrawal of $2, $20, $200, or even $2,000 from the family bank and create a way to multiply the sum at least ten times, then identify a charity they would give the proceeds to, and then observe what happens as a result.

MINOR WITHDRAWAL TURNS TO MAJOR DEPOSIT

From that, our family experienced the miracle of the stained glass stars, thanks to our daughter Mindy and her husband, Brian. At the time they were recently married and just starting out in life. Mindy was pursuing her cosmetology degree, and Brian was in undergraduate studies preparing for medical school. They had very little income or savings. Besides our church, their favorite charity was the Primary Children's Medical Center in Salt Lake City, Utah. This great institution treats thousands of children and will not turn away a patient for lack of financial resources. Mindy called this hospital and found that the previous year, out of thousands of children treated, 144 children didn't make it. They had passed away despite heroic attempts to prolong and save their lives.

Mindy and Brian had gotten an idea from my sister. They learned in an art class how to cut and solder stained glass into beautiful stars, each unique in its own way. Mindy and Brian withdrew $200 from the Legacy Bank to obtain scraps of stained glass, solder, and other materials needed. They dedicated over 150 hours of their time making 144 beautifully unique stars, each dedicated to a child who had passed on. Next, they contacted friends and neighbors for help in purchasing a specially designed (upside-down shaped) Christmas tree. Then the entire family was invited to participate in decorating this stunning tree so it could be auctioned at the annual fundraising Festival of Trees event for Primary Children's Medical Center.

Our family will never forget the unified effort in decorating and contributing to that beautiful tree. At the Festival, hundreds of bidders stopped and gazed in admiration. It was a work of art! Several bids were made until the tree finally sold for $3,800.

It's overwhelming to think that a withdrawal of $200 from the Legacy Bank, combined with hours of selfless service, generated a $3,800 contribution from a young couple that had very little income or savings of their own. The Primary Children's Festival of Trees is now an event that all of our family participates in annually with substantial contributions.

That's not the end of the story. During the ensuing year, Mindy and Brian received orders for hundreds of stained glass stars from individuals, businesses, and gift shops, helping them with much-needed income for sustaining themselves while attending school. The university that Brian was attending invited him to submit a report of the stained glass star Christmas tree project for the children's hospital to its scholarship department. Brian was awarded a handsome scholarship for not only his academic achievements (4.0 GPA), but also for his unselfish contribution to the community.

When you give, the world gives back. Life is truly abundant!

PLANNING YOUR OWN RETREAT

Just imagine the impact Family Retreats with a Purpose could have on your own family. To give you a little jump-start, here's a basic checklist:

- **Location** – Where would you like to hold your upcoming retreat?

- **Duration** – How long would you like your retreat to last?

- **Dates** – When do you want to get away with your family? Consider things like business, school, and sports schedules, but also set expectations that family members will need to prioritize the retreat, which may mean missing out on other activities.

- **Goals** – What are your primary and secondary goals for the retreat?

- **Theme** – What theme will you reinforce throughout the retreat?

- **Participants** – Who will be included? Just adults? Children, as well? Is there a minimum age for young children?

- **Topics** – What topics will you want speakers to cover during devotionals/sessions?

- **Speakers** – Who will teach devotionals/sessions? Will you invite a guest speaker? If so, whom?

- **Legacy Bank Activities** – What type of activities will you engage in to make deposits and withdrawals in the Legacy Bank? I Remember When? What Matters Most? Better Life Circle? Opportunity BREAK-through?

- **Fun** – What type of recreation will be available? Will it be scheduled as a group or individual free time?

- **Roles** – What role does each participant play in the retreat?

- **Agenda** – Don't try winging it—the more focused your agenda, the more successful your retreat will be. What will your agenda include?

- **Communication & Planning** – What type of pre-retreat communication and planning needs to take place? Will there be reading or activity assignments before everyone arrives? How will you communicate retreat itineraries, agenda, goals, etc.?

- **Miscellaneous** – Any other details to plan?

- **Frequency** – How often do you want to hold subsequent retreats?

You can plan the retreat with your spouse, or include other family members in the decision-making process. Make sure to maintain a balance between fun and focus, so everyone can enjoy the retreat as much as they experience personal transformations.

MAKE IT YOUR OWN

I've shared a lot about my own family's Retreats with a Purpose, but keep in mind, as with any aspect of developing Authentic Wealth, it's important to make it your own.

One of our Legacy Coaches, for example, holds much less formal Family Retreats with a Purpose. His children range in age from high school to elementary school, and they dedicate just fifteen minutes each morning to discussions and lessons on their values, good books, etc. (Some mornings the discussions naturally extend to thirty or forty minutes because the children are so engaged.) After the morning session, they head out for a day of fun, and that's the extent of the formal discussion time.

We have clients who, when they first learned about Retreats with a Purpose, didn't have children of their own. They planned a trip with their nieces and nephews—and on the first morning when Uncle Phil started teaching a lesson with a whiteboard, they asked if this was some kind of trick. But Uncle Phil stuck with his purpose-driven agenda, and in the end, all of the nieces and nephews said it was the best trip they'd ever been on. This couple now holds Retreats with a Purpose with their own children, who look forward to it every year.

Another couple implementing our Entitlement Abolition Kit recently tested out their first Retreat with a Purpose. They hosted their grandchildren on a trip to a cabin on the lake, just a couple hours north of Salt Lake City. Their agenda was simple: go get ice cream shakes and, on the way, stop by a special historic/religious site and share their thoughts on family values; go boating; go to a movie; and visit the local cemetery and share inspiring stories about the great-grandparents buried there. The trip was a hit with the grandkids, and they can't wait to add more teaching elements to their plans next summer.

"OTHER FAMILY" RETREATS

As I have mentioned before, "family" is who you define that to be. We describe our company with our wonderful employees as family. Hence we have Business Retreats with a Purpose. Family could be your fellow classmates from school, or it could be a group that you have a certain stewardship for, such as a Scout leader who takes Scouts on camping retreats. Following is an example of one I facilitated.

I served as Scout leader when my sons were Boy Scouts, and I was asked to take a group of ten fourteen- and fifteen-year-old scouts on a high-adventure, wilderness retreat. I accepted, as long as I could conduct it like a Retreat with a Purpose.

I held several planning meetings with the boys and their fathers so that the expectations and anticipation of the trip were as exciting as the trip itself. I led ten boys and five fathers on a four-day, three-night backpacking adventure that started at 7,500 feet above sea level in the Wind River mountain range in Wyoming. It was a grueling three-hour hike where we ascended to 10,500 feet and then trekked down rugged terrain to a remote lake located at 9,500 feet.

At the 10,500-foot summit, we stopped to catch our breath and take in the scenery that would rival any calendar or postcard photo. It was there that I announced to the young men that I wanted them to have a "Four Seasons" experience. I explained the Four Seasons hotel chain has a goal to have its guests always compare any other hotel experience to the Four Seasons—that the Four Seasons sets the highest bar. So I told the young men that for the rest of their lives, whenever they went camping or fishing, I wanted them to compare it back to the time they were age 14 and camped for three nights in the Wind Rivers—the ultimate trip.

I told them: It won't be just the fish you're going to catch (and we caught plenty of fish), or the memory of the challenge of getting into and out of the campsite. You'll remember how you felt about your potential and the clarity you had about your future as we sat around the campfire and talked like men.

The first evening after a dinner of fresh fish tacos, we gathered around the campfire and did the What Matters Most exercise. Basically, they took about fifteen minutes writing down what matters most: to save or preserve, to always remember ... all the way to fight for, sacrifice for, or even die for. They also wrote down what matters most to do every year and why, every quarter and why, every month and why, every week and why, and every day and why. We then went around the circle and everyone shared what mattered most to them. The fathers in attendance were blown away by what the boys articulated.

By the next evening, the boys knew we meant business, and they had all experienced some real hardship of one sort or another during the trip, so the "layers of onion" had been peeled back a bit, and they weren't so concerned about acting macho. After fresh fish and chips we did the Unacceptable Detours & Dead Ends exercise. (*Download and complete your own Unacceptable Detours & Dead Ends exercise at www.EntitlementAbolition.com/Resources.*)

Each participant wrote down at least five "detours or dead ends" they did not want to regret (doing or not doing) at the end of the day (their lives). They then wrote down what would be so unacceptable about the regret. Next they explored what they were going to do over the next ninety days to avoid having such a regret. They also indicated the first action step they were going to take. Again, we went around the circle and shared our feelings. As a father and leader, my buttons almost busted off my shirt in pride and admiration for these young men.

By the third evening they were experts at catching, fileting, and cooking fresh trout—this time with lemon pepper, grilled over the fire. During the final campfire experience, we all filled out our Opportunity BREAK-Through in ten relationships. The framing was this: imagine we are sitting here five years from tonight; what has to have happened for you to be happy with your relationship progress with:

1) God
2) Your parents
3) Your siblings

4) Your friends

5) Your physical well-being

6) Your intellect

7) Your school, job, or profession

8) Your financial self-reliance

9) Church service

10) Community service

They then wrote down the **B**arriers to overcome, the **R**esources to utilize, the **E**xperiences to draw from, the **A**ction steps needed, and the **K**nowledge to garner in order to see it come to fruition. And one last time we went around the circle and shared.

The boys were on a natural high the next day as we cleaned up camp and hiked back to our vehicles. When the boys arrived back home late that evening, their parents asked, "So how was it?" Instead of the normal grunt and escape to the bedroom, the parents reported that every boy burst through the door energized and stayed up past midnight talking about all of the experiences they had. Some parents said their sons wouldn't stop talking about the trip for several weeks.

I received a thank-you letter from every boy—and they weren't just a sentence or two—the average letter was at least one or two pages in length! One set of parents said the retreat was a game-changer for their son—he came out of his shell, improved his grades dramatically, kept his goals on his bedroom mirror for the entire year, and followed through with them.

Again, this is an example of consciously training the mind and body to unconsciously act in harmony with your values and vision. For me as a leader, it was the best way to be "sincerely interested" in these young men, as I will explain at the end of Chapter 11.

Whatever you do, however you strategize your retreat … don't wait. Start planning now for your own Retreats with a Purpose. If it's with community or work groups, leverage the opportunity to grow closer, to redefine what matters most to the organization and to the individuals involved. If it's with your family, use the retreats as an opportunity to add to your Legacy Bank. Share memories from those that have wisdom, teach principles that lay a foundation for real prosperity, and most of all, make sure those around you know how much you love them.

chapter 8
Grandpa's Camp

> " *Nobody can do for little children what grandparents can do. Grandparents sort of sprinkle stardust over the lives of little children.*"
>
> *Alex Haley*

Imagine a place where grandchildren and grandparents come together every year. A time where only fun, imagination, and unforgettable lessons exist. Where there's laughter, adventure, and bonding. That's Grandpa's Camp, and it's one of my greatest joys in life—and highest recommendations for you to consider adopting in your own family.

For us it has been an invaluable experience, full of incredible memories, and lasting life lessons. Take for example, one of our recent annual themes: Liberty. Throughout our teaching sessions, we focused on the US Constitution and stories about the Founding Fathers—their strong character, guiding influence, and sacrifices. We looked at ways our grandchildren can preserve liberty in their own lives—both on a personal level through making wise choices, as well as by helping protect the nation's liberties.

It is rewarding to see grandchildren's eyes light up when they understand new concepts. It's even more exciting to watch them share what they've learned with their parents (we have parents and young children come the last night) and see that the lessons have made an impression.

Now before you think Grandpa's Camp is all learning and no play, think again. Each day is jam-packed with everything from games and arts and crafts, to four-wheeling, rifle shooting, bows and arrows, hiking, and relaxing. We also have Grandpa's Treehouse, which is our luxury hideaway in the treetops, with air conditioning, swings, and nonstop fun. There's also zip lining, which has a story behind it … one that has since become one of our family's favorite I Remember When stories.

A couple years ago, I told my wife, "Honey, we've got to have a zip line!" With Sharee's thumbs up, I went online and began the research. I found it: the Alien Flier.

It arrived—looking like it was going to be a beauty. Now two days before Grandpa's Camp, I was up there installing the zip line. I got just about everything in place: the platform, the line, the flier, and our back-up safety system—strong bungee cords designed to stop you before you hit the tree at the bottom (in case the brakes don't do their job). One thing I didn't figure I needed for the test run was the handlebars— I could just hang on the brakes if I needed to, right?

Well, by now it was close to the time I had to head back down to Salt Lake City to volunteer at the boys' and girls' home. With about fifteen minutes before I needed to leave, I was thinking it would be a brilliant idea to have Grandpa test the zip line before the grandkids came up.

I launched out and all of a sudden, I started zipping, and I mean zipping. About halfway down, I did the math. The grandkids' average weight was sixty-five to eighty pounds. Grandpa was 165 pounds. Turns out you don't need much of a slope (and I had a decent one) to get velocity. And it also turns out they make those handlebars for a good reason. If you don't have anything to hold onto for leverage, well, let's just say it's ugly.

I grabbed the brakes and held on for dear life—they started smoking. The end of the line was coming at me, faster and faster, and I was thinking, "I'm so glad I installed those bungee cords!"

Well, I learned a few things: 1) They don't call it zip for nothing; 2) While you CAN hold onto the brakes, if you don't want to burn through them before you approach the end of the line, you would rather have handlebars; 3) Even though bungee cords can be strong, they're not strong enough to stop a grown man hurtling down the zip line with burned-out brakes; and 4) If you MUST hit the tree at the bottom due to high personal velocity and useless bungee cords, it would have been wise to wear a helmet.

Yep, I hit the cords, the tree, the deck … and saw stars. I was all alone. I finally got myself to my car to assess the damages. I guess it could have been worse: one big toe nail torn clean off (even inside my shoe!) that took more than a year to grow back, a nasty mark on my forehead that stayed around for the better part of a month (despite constant applications of essential oils), and a few bumps and bruises. Dumbest thing I've done in a long time.

Two days later, it was safe for the grandkids. I changed the angle, added those darn handlebars, and replaced the brakes. My grandkids love the story because it proves "even ol' grandpa doesn't think sometimes!"

PLANNING CAMP ACTIVITIES

At our Grandpa's Camp, we like to plan each day so it has a mix of all the right ingredients: learning, fun, food, and sharing. The first couple of days is for grandkids twelve years old and up. This is high-level learning and high-level play (repelling, four-wheeling, etc.). Then Days 3 and 4, the eight-to-eleven year-olds join us and learn from the older cousins. Days 5 and 6, the little ones, four-to-seven years old, attend, and we do more arts and crafts and simple activities. Finally, on the evening of Day 6, the parents and toddlers join us to share in dinner, campfire activities and a final sleepover. Sometimes we divide up this six days over two weekends to give ourselves a breather.

We often use mealtimes and campfires as teaching times. For example, here's what we taught at a recent camp:

- Day 1 Campfire – religious beliefs with bedtime stories
- Day 2 Breakfast – maximizing our talents and unique abilities
- Day 2 Lunch – how money works
- Day 2 Dinner – our heritage, relatives, and ancestors
- Day 3 Breakfast – serving others
- Day 3 Lunch – health, diet, and exercise
- Day 3 Campfire – I Remember When stories

In between mealtimes, we rotate between arts and crafts (grandchildren are assigned to lead one of these craft sessions themselves) and fun activities (hikes, zip lining, ATVs, etc.).

Just as with Family Retreats with a Purpose, there's no one set way to plan your grandparents' camp, or just one venue that works. You only need a few basics:

- **Distraction-Free Zone** – Whether it's your home, a cabin, or a campground, hold your camp at a venue that allows you all to get away from day-to-day distractions.

- **Overnight Accommodations** – Overnight stays aren't absolutely necessary, but it helps kids and grandparents bond if everyone's not leaving in the evening for sports or lessons or other duties. We tend to go for four days, three nights.

- **Lots of Fun** – Fun is critical, but that can take any form. You don't need ATVs, snowmobiles, or zip lines. Simple activities like croquet, water balloon volleyball, sack races, board game championships, arts and crafts, and more can add to the joy of the event.

- **Delicious Food** – From foil dinners cooked in the fire coals, to fruit crepes, to tri-tip on the grill, we make sure the food is something the kids look forward to. Serve up whatever your brood likes, and they'll be coming back for more.

- **Theme & Meaningful Lessons** – Utilize your time together to reinforce principles that are in line with your family's values and vision, and that reinforce the Three Dimensions of Authentic Wealth (Financial, Intellectual and Foundational).

Foundational Dimension discussions could be on what values are or what it means to eat healthy. Intellectual Dimension discussions could be about what their favorite subjects are in school (what are they good at doing), or family traditions they like (or would like to have). Financially, discussions can be centered on how to sacrifice what you want now for the things you really want in the future, or how to pay it forward by contributing money, time, or talents to others who are less fortunate.

- Pre-Event Preparation – Along with the logistics planning you and your spouse will do, you'll want your grandchildren to prepare for the lessons and activities you'll be leading. We send around a list of "homework" assignments for our grandchildren to accomplish with their parents a few weeks beforehand.

  Prior to Grandpa's Camp, we assign certain activities and preparation. One year, the following assignments were made for each child to complete before the camp to align with the purposes for each day:

1) Create and come with a simple photo album with pictures of your relatives and ancestors, and be prepared to tell a story about one of your grandparents.

2) Complete an aptitude questionnaire, and be prepared to share what it is you like to do.

3) Visit one of your parents' workplaces, and be prepared to share what your mom or dad does to provide for the family.

4) Go on a grocery shopping trip with your mom or dad, and be prepared to explain how to best use a limited amount of money and identify the difference between needs and wants.

5) Perform one act of kindness for each member of your family, and be prepared to share how you felt doing it.

- **Age Limits** – We've found that any younger than about four years old makes participation tough, so that's our minimum age limit, and we bring the grandchildren in waves, based on age. Identify what works best for you and your family.

- **Sharing the Learning** – We have grandkids of all ages—from preschoolers on up to teenagers. We've found it helps to teach some principles to the older kids, and have them in turn teach the younger kids. On that last night when the parents and tiny ones join us, the older kids share what they've been learning.

- **Next Time?** – Decide how often you'll hold grandparents' camp. For us, this is annually, but it could be semi-annually, quarterly, etc.

You can find a sample of a Grandpa's Camp Agenda at www. EntitlementAbolition.com/Resources.

EVEN LEARNING CAN BE FUN

With fourteen grandchildren, it's probably obvious that it's not all necessarily smooth sailing at Grandpa's Camp. There are definitely times when the older children aren't as excited as the younger children to apply glue, glitter, and pizzazz to an arts and crafts project.

We've honed our agenda over the years to attune the activities to the different age groups and attention spans. And we've headed off the "I'm boooooored!" complaints by involving the older children as mentors and assistants to the younger ones, assigning them opportunities to lead lessons and activities. For example, on the final two days when the four-year-olds finally arrive, the favorite activity has been our annual treasure hunt. Now we assign the teenaged grandchildren to plan and conduct the treasure hunt, and it has become an incredible "everyone involved" experience.

We've also seen the impact of object lessons that help set the tone for a peaceful six days. For example, one year Sharee and I filled a Mason jar with water from the lake and added a good scoop of sand from the shore.

We explained that, "Sometimes when we get frustrated or mad at each other, we can feel like this!" We shook the jar, which turned the water nearly opaque with swirling mud. "This is 'muddy mind,' and it's what happens when we let ourselves get upset."

We asked them what would happen if we let it settle. They watched the granules descend to the bottom of the jar, and the water became clear again. "This is clear mind. When we're at Grandpa's Camp, it's important to remember that if you feel like you have muddy mind, it's best to wait until it settles and you have clear mind. Then you can talk to your cousin, brother, or sister about your challenge, to work it out." They still talk about muddy mind and clear mind at family dinners today!

BUILD ANTICIPATION AND REMINISCE OFTEN

If you recollect from your own childhood, usually the anticipation of a trip was as exciting (or more exciting) than the actual trip. We announce the date of Grandpa's Camp six months in advance, at Christmas time. The grandchildren know the theme and their assignments to teach ninety days out and can begin planning their activity or art/craft project. Just as children begin asking, "How much lawwwnger?" or "Are we theeeeere yet?" when you've only been on the road thirty minutes of a five-hour drive, the grandchildren will be peppering their moms and dads with, "How many more days 'til Grandpa's Camp?"

My daughter-in-law, Harmony, came up with a brilliant idea before the first camp that they continue to this day. With her son, Ethan (and now joined by younger sister, Taylor), they make a "Grandpa's Camp Chain" out of construction paper with links for every day of each month (different colors for each month) to hang all around their bedrooms. Each day, they get to cut off one of the links so they can physically see how many days are left until Grandpa's Camp. The chain starts out with 180-plus links! Harmony also has them decorate the specific links for other holidays, birthdates and family activities. The anticipation for Grandpa's Camp becomes even more heightened.

That next Christmas after our first camp, Ethan couldn't wait to have me open a big gift box he had wrapped—my very own twenty-four-foot Grandpa's Camp Chain to hang in our sunroom, so even *Grandpa* wouldn't forget.

One strategic by-product of Grandpa's Camp is that our married children use the time while their children are being "tended" by Grandma and Grandpa to schedule their own husband and wife retreats (which we highly encourage them to do), or to complete projects that are normally hard to do while the kids are around.

A couple of times a year, as grandparents, we also have a sleepover at our house, treehouse, or cabin to enjoy and bond with our grandchildren, build camaraderie among cousins, and give their parents another break for a "date night." It's also a wonderful way to reminisce about the previous camp—looking back at photos, sharing I Remember When memories—and gather ideas for the next camp.

You can make these intermittent grandchildren gatherings fun. For example, this year, Sharee and I will be hosting a spaghetti dinner night with our grandchildren where they will all put on a white T-shirt and plastic surgical gloves. There will be one rule: eat your spaghetti and meatballs using only your hands—no utensils! (Of course, this dinner will be held outdoors!)

As some of our grandchildren are now entering their dating years, we plan to host a candlelight dinner at our home for each grandchild and a date (along with a few of their friends and their dates) for one of their formal school dances. With Sharee as the cook and me as the butler/waiter (dressed in a tuxedo), we want our grandchildren to remember the awesome dinner date where they were given the royal treatment at "Grandma and Grandpa's Bistro."

GO CAMPING ... NOW

Some of our best memories have come from our camps. There's nothing like getting away to just spend time together, reinforce what's important, and simply have fun. Earlier in the book, I mentioned the butterflies we watched emerge while at camp. Priceless. Our grandkids are all still talking about that.

I would recommend whatever you do, however you plan it is great—just don't wait. Overall, we have precious few days with our grandchildren, especially during the years they are open to listening to their grandparents. So don't waste the opportunity. Start today to plan your camp, and you'll be thrilled with the results.

chapter 9
Managing
KASH

" Each day of our lives we make deposits in the memory banks of our children."

Charles R. Swindoll

Jobs were scarce when I was in my early and mid-teens. As a young boy I had delivered the Orem *Geneva Times* newspaper, picked cherries for Farley's orchards, and I worked grinding and buffing the metal ears on ski bindings for Miller Ski Company in Orem. On occasion, I would work sun up to sun down in Schofield or Alberta helping brand sheep or building miles of fencing on Cal Jacob's sheep ranch to earn $20 a day.

In 1968, a new Kentucky Fried Chicken franchise was built in Orem, and it paid somewhat better ($1.25 per hour) than McDonald's or the "Hi Spot" hamburger drive-ins where my brother Sherm and sisters, Glenda and Diana, had worked. The problem was, Donald Tuft, the new owner, only needed three chicken cooks at the outset, and more than 150 boys lined up to interview for the job. I was elated when I learned that I was selected for the job, along with two other boys. I was a few months away from sixteen years old at the time, and the job required a food-handler's permit which was not normally available until age 16. The county health department made an exception for me, so I took the class and certified. Mr. Tuft told me that I was the only boy that had left him a resume, and on the resume it revealed that I was an Eagle Scout. That impressed him, and he hired me.

I was extremely grateful for the job opportunity and worked very hard to do my best. I held the record for cooking the most pressure cookers of chicken by myself, and was eventually promoted to assistant manager (which meant managing some of my friends who were ahead of me in high school—luckily they were respectful).

One night, some of the chicken cooks informed me that the new diagonal road going from Orem into Provo was finished and opened. It had an overpass road going over it. This was unique because I-15 had not yet been constructed, and overpasses were only to be found on California freeways or on a few train tracks in Lindon and Murray, Utah. They suggested that we hurry and close up KFC that night and go down to the new overpass and toss some eggs at cars as they went under us. I knew better, but I wanted to be cool with these older schoolmates. So we cleaned up at closing and took thirty eggs with us. We got our kicks tossing them over the overpass at passing cars. To my knowledge, we didn't hit any, but we saw a few brake lights go on.

I got home that evening—no later than I usually arrived—but my mother had intuition like you wouldn't believe. She knew when her boys Sherm and Doug were up to "no good." My mother and father were waiting in the living room for me, and as I opened the living room door they asked, "Doug, where have you been?"

I had learned earlier in life that if I lied, I would get into deeper yogurt. I felt really stupid as I blurted out, "Uh, I've been down on the new overpass going into Provo throwing eggs at cars!" My confession sounded so idiotic. My father got up from his chair, walked over and put his arm around me and said, "Son, we thought we could trust you!" I had let them down. My father saying that made me feel like a dagger had pierced my chest. Then he said, "Let's go for a ride." I asked, "Where to?" My father said, "To the Orem City Police Department—you're going to turn yourself in."

That was the longest ride ever! About a month earlier, when I closed up KFC the night before the 4th of July (the biggest day of the year for KFC), the store had been burglarized. It was an inside job, because the door was still locked the next morning, and the thieves had hauled out a 300-pound safe full of cash by pouring grease all over the floor. Sergeant Francis Fillmore, one of twenty-seven police officers on Orem's department, called and informed me that the store had been burglarized during the night, but assured me that the owner said I was one of the most impeccably honest young men he had ever met. He just wanted to conduct a routine interview with me and then I could enjoy the holiday (as I was not scheduled to work until 4 pm that day).

Well, I was hoping that Sergeant Francis Fillmore was not on swing shift that night because I was so embarrassed. Who greeted me at 11 pm at the police station? Sergeant Francis Fillmore! He said, "Well, Doug Andrew, what brings you here this hour of the night?" I sheepishly replied, "Well sir, I have a confession to make."

He escorted me into the police station interrogation room where a green lamp was hanging from the ceiling and the fingerprint pads were ready. He said, "Proceed!" I then proceeded to tell him about the egg tossing caper, and he let out a big sigh! He thought I had come to confess that I was involved in the burglary! He was totally relieved that I had only been tossing eggs at cars. Then my father asked Sergeant Fillmore to explain to me what could have happened if I would have caused an accident, and I heard phrases like "involuntary manslaughter." I rode home with my dad that night and thanked him for loving me enough to turn me in to the cops. I knew this would be a story I would tell my own children someday—and I have numerous times and to other youth as well. Believe me, I did other stupid things in my youth—but nothing that stupid again!

This is one of the stories I've shared at our Family Retreats with a Purpose—and it's by far one of my grandkids' favorites. They giggle to imagine Grandpa doing something so—well, just plain dumb. Along with it being a good tale, it also gives me the chance to reinforce some Andrew family values:

- **Work ethic** – Sharing insights on my early jobs helps them see how important it is to work hard and prove yourself.

- **Honesty** – When I recount how I fessed up to my parents, the grandkids recognize no matter how hard it may be, honesty is indeed the best policy.

- **Accountability** – When I share this powerful lesson my father taught me in going to the police, they understand the importance of dealing "above the line" with accountability.

With just one story, I've accomplished several important objectives, *and* we've had fun. We call this kind of storytelling activity: I Remember When. It's a simple but powerful tool for managing the KASH in life.

LEGACY BANK DEPOSITS

In Chapters 5 and 6, I introduced the concept of the Legacy Bank, and talked about the importance of making deposits and withdrawals in your family's bank, outlining your KASH Blueprint, and creating your values and vision. In Chapters 7 and 8, I shared how to plan Retreats with a Purpose and Grandpa's Camp—two powerful events that can help you and your family set aside time to make KASH deposits in your Legacy Bank.

When I introduce the Legacy Bank, many people get a confused look on their faces and ask, "What are you talking about?" As a reminder, the Legacy Bank is a metaphor—it's not a chartered bank down the street—but a conceptual bank. It's where you and your family capture your **K**nowledge, the gems of wisdom that you've learned through your life experiences, education, and professional pursuits.

You also invest the **A**ttitudes that you've developed about life; about the Universe, God, or a Higher Power; about work ethic; about relationships; essentially—about everything.

Then you share your **S**kills and Unique Ability®. It could be an appreciation for music or entrepreneurial strategies. It could be great technique in sports or things you've mastered in exercise and wellness.

Finally, you pass along your **H**abits—maybe you're early risers who set aside time each morning for meditation or prayer, reading good books, and exercise. Or perhaps it's traditions or cultural customs you maintain. Maybe it's getting on a Win Streak, or capturing life's hard-won lessons with The Better Life Circle.

Whatever it is, your family's goal should be to harness all of that KASH so that future generations will be able to build on what you've deposited and continue on in the Abundance Cycle, rather than dropping back to the Scarcity Cycle and starting from scratch.

In this chapter, we're going to discuss some of the strategies I've found for capturing these important deposits.

I REMEMBER WHEN

Earlier in this book I introduced the concept of I Remember When stories. To help explain it further, as we go through life, whether it's at work or home, with friends or extended family, we all have unique experiences. Some are uplifting, others are defining, and some are just plain funny. But what often happens? Life keeps zipping by, and these great moments slip to the back of our minds. They might become fuzzy, or we might forget them altogether. But what if we kept them fresh, shared them, and they could keep giving their energy and insight for years to come?

The I Remember When activity is something we do regularly with our children and grandchildren—it's one of the highlights of our Family Retreats with a Purpose. I Remember When has made all the difference in how we've grown closer, preserved precious memories and, really, just had a blast together.

Here's how it works: Everyone comes prepared with at least three I Remember When stories. These can include just about anything—

overcoming personal challenges, a "first" in life, great advice someone gave, fun times shared, or even most embarrassing moments.

Everyone types them out and brings a printed copy, as well as a copy on a thumb drive (if you have young children, they can share them aloud and someone can write them down, or you can record them live and transcribe the stories later). The stories are kept brief, each about 750 words or less. Then as you gather, you take turns sharing the stories. When done, not only have you just spent unforgettable time laughing, listening, and growing closer, but you can compile the stories into a binder, and instantly, you've just begun building a written history … in a really easy way! *(Download the I Remember When tool at www. EntitlementAbolition.com/Resources.)*

When our family first started doing this, I came up with a list of seventy-seven memories or defining moments in my life. I've added forty or fifty since then, and our children and grandchildren absolutely love these moments. They seem to especially like the one about the night my father had me turn myself into the police.

Another favorite is when I talked about "When wisdom calls, don't give it a busy signal." I had five different examples of how I was motivated to do something, and when wisdom knocked, I didn't turn away; I pursued the endeavor, and it brought great blessings.

The grandkids have also loved the story of the Mysterious Walnut. When I was a child, during the Thanksgiving and Christmas holidays, my mom would put out a wooden tray filled with nuts and a nutcracker. One day when no one was looking, I took a walnut, cracked it open perfectly along the natural seam and removed the nutmeat from one side. Then I got into the fridge and snuck a fat red rubber band off the celery. I glued the rubber band to the empty half of the shell, sealed the walnut shut with the glue, and slid it back onto the nut tray. I smiled at my work—the perfect prank.

Well, my Dad took a handful of nuts in his lunch one day to work at Geneva Steel. He was cracking away when he discovered the rubber band. "Hey look at this!" he said as he showed it to one of the guys. His co-worker was fascinated … he was sure this rubber band had somehow flipped into the walnut tree during the blossoming stage. He asserted it must have been naturally grafted inside the walnut during the nut's development, so he took the mysterious walnut to the agriculture department at nearby Brigham Young University. They studied it and reported the phenomenon to the Provo Daily Herald newspaper, which wrote up a small article about this freak of nature.

I remember hearing Dad read the paper, chuckling with pride as he pointed out the article to my mom. I was sitting in the living room, and my face turned white. I thought I was in deep trouble for causing all of that hoopla. I finally got the courage to confess what I had done to my dad, thinking I was maybe going to have to go to court or apologize publicly to the newspaper or BYU's agriculture department. He just laughed and made me feel pretty good about pulling off a caper like that. He wasn't sure he was going to tell his fellow worker that it was all a little boy's joke.

We've shared lots of funny stories like these over the years, like the time we were at Disneyland, and my son Emron was in line for the bobsleds doing tricks on the handrail. He fell and did a face plant in the petunias as we were ready to get on. But the I Remember When stories also get touching and uplifting, like when my children talk about the value of hard work or how they met their spouses.

This activity has since extended from my own family and employees to now my siblings. At our annual get-together at our cabin, all the siblings and spouses bring three stories. We start sharing over dinner Sunday night, then keep the stories going over breakfast and even lunch the next day. There are currently ten of us, so we end up gathering thirty stories total. Imagine what that will be when we do this over five years—150 stories! It will be a book our children and grandchildren will treasure forever. It's probably the most impactful twenty-four hours we invest together as adult siblings each year.

Inevitably during I Remember When sessions, the grandchildren will start peppering the storyteller with questions—some are easy, like "How did you meet Grandma?" and some make you blush, like "Grandpa, did you ever kiss a girl on the first date?" or "Have you ever been in a fist fight?"

In fact, questions are a great way to spur I Remember When stories. Here is a basic list of questions to get you and your group started. Have everyone pick two to three for your first session, then answer more at future gatherings.

- As a child or teen, what recognition did you receive (at school, sports, etc.), and how did that impact your life?

- What is something a school teacher taught that you've never forgotten?

- Are there any memorable experiences from sports (or music or other talent development) that helped shape your life?

- What was your best friend like growing up? What were some of your capers together? What did you learn from him/her?

- When and how did you meet your spouse?

- What was your first job? What did you like/not like about it? What did it teach you?

- How did you learn the value of hard work?

- Did you ever let someone down when they were counting on you? How did you feel? What did you learn?

- Have you come through for someone when they were counting on you? How did you feel? What did you learn?

- What are some of your fondest holiday memories?

- What are some of your favorite family traditions?

- What memorable family trips did you take? How did they touch your life?

- What are things your mom and dad (or grandparents) used to always say? How did that shape you?

- What are some things you and your siblings would do behind your parents' backs?

- Was there ever a time when you were telling the truth and no one would believe you?

- How about a time when you told a fib, then learned from it?

- Have you ever worked hard for something and didn't get it … or did?

- How and when did you learn that Santa Claus and the Easter Bunny weren't real? (Spoiler alert: don't share this one around young children who still believe!)

- What kind of technology (or lack thereof) did you enjoy as a kid?

- Were there ever any "close calls" where you could have ended up "six-feet under" but came out alive?

I would encourage you to take the I Remember When activity into your workplace and family life. Plan Retreats with a Purpose. Encourage everyone to bring stories, and watch the magic that happens. Keep the recorded stories where everyone can return to them and read them (consider emailing an electronic version around, as well).

CAPTURING LIFE SKETCHES

My dad was one of my heroes—he taught me to work hard; he taught me responsibility; and he taught me accountability.

As my dad was advancing in age, my brother Sherm and I didn't want to let time go by without connecting, so we scheduled regular lunches with my dad. We would laugh and share stories, which we began to record during our lunch sessions.

Then we wanted to take it to the next level—to go from casual I Remember When chats to actually capturing his life sketch. My dad wasn't a writer—but he was a great talker. So my wife, Sharee, and I invited my dad and his sweet companion, Mary Deane, (who joined him after my mom passed away), to join us in Hawaii for a getaway.

The one caveat? I promised him we would go out to dinner at a fantastic restaurant every night, provided he answered the memory jogging questions I gave him for the day. He agreed, so every day I'd "trap" him in a room, and we'd dive into tales of his life. It was fascinating. We covered:

1. Ancestry
2. Early childhood
3. Courtship years
4. Early married life and child-rearing
5. Empty-nester stage
6. Church service
7. Professional and community service

I simply asked him to read the question into a recorder and just talk about the answer. We uncovered great gems, like the story of his family's Model T Ford. Here's an excerpt from that discussion:

I remember riding to Salt Lake, and my parents had a Model T Ford. As a boy, I always sat in the front seat with my father, and my mother and sister always rode in the backseat. It was a two-lane cement road all the way to Springville and on to Salt Lake. It took two hours to ride to Salt Lake, especially in the winter time. In the winter time the heater in the car was just a manifold heater. It was just a little plate in the floorboard where the heat would come up from the exhaust inside the motor.

So my parents would always have bricks; they would heat bricks and wrap them in newspaper so we could put our feet on them to keep warm. We would have one for each of us riding in the car. Then of course when we would get to Salt Lake, we would put these bricks on the coal stove and get them good and hot to come back home and keep our feet warm while traveling.

These cars didn't have glass windows—they had these portable things that would snap on with a little twist to keep the wind out and try to keep it warm. We had that Model T Ford a number of years. Later on my father got a new car. It was an Overland. It was a 1925. I think it cost $700 brand new. He had that a number of years until I finally got old enough *to drive, and he let me take it a couple three times to drive it on some of my first dates. It had a gear shift, you know. And that's the first time I learned how to drive a car with a gear shift.*

In one week we captured 130 pages of his life sketch, then added photos and published his book, titled, *Glenn Andrew, A Man of Steel*—because he was a superintendent at US Steel Geneva Works during his career.

We printed the book, then copied it in digital form, along with video and audio from our many interviews, and burned that to hundreds of CDs and DVDs for about thirty-four cents apiece in replication costs. We distributed them to family and friends at his funeral. That was more valuable than if every child and grandchild had inherited a quarter of a million dollars!

Now that he is gone, I wonder what would have happened if we hadn't taken the time to capture his experiences, stories, and wisdom. They would have gone to his grave with him. Now they will live on forever, benefiting his posterity.

As I look back, it all started with those lunches. I have to admit—there were many of those Fridays that I had a lot going on in my own life. So did Sherm. But we kept those appointments with Dad, even though he would always reassure us that he understood if we needed a raincheck.

Little did I know it wasn't just my dad that I would be grateful I was connecting with. Sherm and I were fortunate to log over one hundred of those Friday lunches with our dad before March 10, 1999. On that date in the evening, the phone rang about 11:45 pm (not a good sign when someone calls that late).

On the other end was Sue, Sherm's wife, sobbing. The Highway Patrol had just left her home informing her that Sherm has been killed in a one-car rollover while traveling on a business trip toward Nevada. I couldn't believe it. Immediately Sharee and I drove to their home to help comfort Sue.

All along I thought we were going to outlast Dad, but those hundred lunches also gave me extra time with my brother, who had always been one of my best friends. How grateful I was to have gotten together with the guy who had charisma like you wouldn't believe, who was always there for others. Who knew he would "graduate" before me and even Dad?!

Dad and I were fortunate to enjoy about another fifty Friday lunches together before he passed on in 2004. Two of my favorite lunch buddies are now gone. I will never regret taking time to be with Sherm and Dad. That time was so much more valuable than any other to-do's I could have crossed off.

I'm sure you have loved ones whose stories and life lessons could bless your family and friends. If wisdom is calling right now, don't give it a busy signal. Don't let time get away from you. Avoid big regrets and schedule time to capture what they have to say. Ask them questions and record their answers. Recording is easier than ever with built-in apps on smart phones—and keep in mind some people do better if the recording device is out of sight, perhaps on your lap, so they feel like they're just talking off the cuff.

But don't stop there. Put it on paper and share it at your next family gathering (or email it to everyone). If no one in the family is fond of typing, there are affordable transcription services with companies like www.rev.com that will transcribe for you.

And remember to do more than just capture the stories. Bring them out, read them, share them. At your next Family Retreat with a Purpose, for example, you could ask a family member to pick one story from your family's archive to present to the group. This way the stories and lessons are alive and well—becoming "withdrawals" from your Legacy Bank that can go on and compound in value for your children and grandchildren.

MEMORY-JOGGER QUESTIONS

For about five years, I had a church stewardship responsibility to over-see the welfare of twenty-seven widows, widowers, and elderly cou-ples who might need help with various tasks such as yard cleanup, furnace and air conditioning servicing, and other seasonal chores. We also had a tradition to hold an "empty-nester" gathering at one of the homes once per month to visit, to eat and share, and to help keep tabs on everyone. I put together a two-page outline of "memory-jog-ger" questions and would pick one of the attendees to interview each month. It was a major hit.

I would bring a digital recorder and sometimes a video camera to re-cord the interview. Most went about forty-five minutes, with some ex-tending to nearly two hours. The best ones were unrehearsed, where I just asked them memory joggers in an extemporaneous format. Their children and grandchildren would sometimes attend.

I then took the digital recording and duplicated it on CDs or DVDs for their families. Many times their families requested twenty to thirty cop-ies. They loved hearing the interview wherein their parent or grandpar-ent shared stories in their own voice—many stories which the family had never before heard. I got numerous thank you notes from families for doing this with their loved one. It was amazing to me how many families said that the life sketch captured by me became the primary source for the tribute at the funeral when their parent/grandparent passed on.

The key here is not to worry about getting the entire life history record-ed by voice. The family will treasure just a one- to two-hour recording of the actual voice telling some of the favorite stories. I've done this enough to get pretty good at it. Let me share a secret. Don't stress out the person being interviewed by having them think that they have to prepare for weeks for the interview. I've had some procrastinate it for months and then it became too late as they suffered a stroke or passed away without capturing anything.

It's also how you ask the questions that matters. For example, if you ask them, "So what are your talents and unique abilities?" 90% of the time, they will say, "Oh, I don't have any talents!" Rather, you ask, "So Fred, if you had your druthers, and time, energy, and resources were not an issue, *what would you choose to do more of?*" Now they will tell you their talents.

I remember sitting in the living room of a sweet eighty-seven-year-old woman whose husband had just passed away the previous year. In her home were more than one hundred hand-painted porcelain dolls—all with outfits sewn by her. She had oil paintings, cross-stitch pillows and needle-point-covered stools she had created. I can assure you that if I had asked her what her talents were, she would have declared that she didn't have any. But all I had to ask was, "So, if time, energy and resources were not an issue, what would you choose to do more of?" And she went on exuberantly for five minutes about how she would make additional porcelain dolls depicting Elsa and Anna from the movie, *Frozen,* a cross-stitch pillow case for her great-grandchildren, several more oil paintings, and so forth.

I've also learned that you need to warm them up with some easy questions first, and then toward the end of the interview you can get to the real gems that will be treasured forever. For example, I usually start out with questions about where they were born, their earliest memories of childhood, their favorite holidays, how they met their spouse, why they fell in love with their spouse, their first job, when they learned the value of hard work, the schools they attended, favorite subjects, teachers, hobbies, friends, embarrassing moments, etc.

After the warm-up and they are relaxed, you can begin asking them questions like:

- What do you appreciate about each of your children?
- Will you share some of your personal victories and/or defeats and what you learned?

- Who had a significant impact in your life and why?

- What were your favorite traditions?

- What are you most passionate about right now?

- What do you love about life?

- What do you want to accomplish before you leave this world?

- What's worth sacrificing for?

- What's worth fighting for?

- What's worth dying for?

- What are you most grateful for?

- What do you believe to be true?

- What would you like your posterity to remember?

It's the final ten to fifteen minutes of the interview that brings tears to the one sharing, and especially to his or her loved ones.

In our Entitlement Abolition Kit, I include a copy of my entire Memory Jogger Questionnaire. This single activity has become a priceless treasure cherished by many families and will be for generations. JUST DO IT!

QUICK THINKING

One of the greatest gifts we can give our posterity is the habit of consistently envisioning a brighter future—and knowing how to pursue it. One of the tools that I use with my family is the Quick Thinker, a strategy shared with me by Strategic Coach and friend Dan Sullivan. With the Quick Thinker, you:

1. Choose the future you want – three goals, experiences, or achievements that you want in the days or years ahead

2. Decide what part of the past gets to come along – three elements, memories, or traditions that can empower you to stop beating yourself up over mistakes and build on positive experiences

3. Utilize the present to make the best possible progress – three current opportunities that you can leverage to move forward

As an example, here are Quick Thinker categories I recently filled out:

- **Choose the future you want** – *Sharee and I to stay in top physical shape and practice nutritional, healthy habits to increase our life expectancy and enhance our quality of life.*

- **Decide what part of the past gets to come along** – *Appreciation for the experiences (both good and bad) that have transformed our lives to increase the value by helping others and fully understanding how to assist others to overcome their challenges.*

- **Utilize the present to make the best possible progress** – *Use the Solution Formulator, Better Life Circle, Opportunity Breakthrough, Appreciation Accelerator, Project Clarifier, Goal Activator and other Live Abundant tools to enhance the KASH in our family Legacy Bank in perpetuity.*

It sounds so simple, but this process is transformative. It's been a tremendous tool for my family, my employees, and even the youth my wife and I volunteer with at the detention center. They've shared future goals like, "I want to be a father," and "I want to have a great job," or "I want to seize an opportunity to work at a restaurant, rather than go back to my gang." They are consciously training their minds and bodies to unconsciously act in harmony with their values and vision for a brighter future—the bigger picture. It becomes super clear that they need to change who they're hanging out with.

I have observed that a keen moral and ethical mindset is governed by a sense or perception of the long-term effects or consequences of an action. If a person steals from, kills, or rapes another individual, they rarely are thinking of the consequences or results beyond the instant gratification or anger response of that moment. Hence, when they do what normal society calls "stupid things," it's because they were only thinking of the short-term, brief immediate thrill or gratification without considering the long-term effects.

I recently had one of the counselors approach me, saying, "Whatever you did with the kids—that card you had them fill out? That stayed on the mirror in their cell for an entire month; their demeanor has started to change."

One of the boys I worked with a while ago shared with me that he achieved a Quick Thinker goal—he's now a manager at a restaurant. Another told me his Quick Thinker card helped him adjust how he was behaving, which earned him an early release. Others have shared that they're now focusing on graduating from high school while in lock-down, and they're preparing a resume for a job so they'll be ready to move forward as soon as they are out.

If this exercise can help kids in the darkest of circumstances, imagine what it can do for your own family. Set aside time to have everyone in the family complete The Quick Thinker exercise, then encourage them to share their thoughts on one of their "brighter future" goals. It can help bring everyone together in an abundance mindset, with family members offering support for each other as they pursue that goal.

COMPOUND YOUR KASH

There are other tools I've mentioned that are powerful ways to capture your family's KASH, which include The Better Life Circle, The Solution Formulator, The Appreciation Accelerator, The Negative Experience Transformer. These and other tools are included in modules of the Entitlement Abolition Kit. *(Try some of our most popular tools at www. EntitlementAbolition.com/Resources.)*

But however you approach growing your KASH—whether it's with these tools, I Remember When stories, life sketches, Quick Thinkers or you come up with your own—just be sure to make it a priority. And then make sure to compound its value by sharing your family's stories and insights on a regular basis, encouraging family members to incorporate the lessons learned from each other.

Capitalizing on your KASH is just as integral to the abundance of future generations as capitalizing on your cash. So invest time now, and enjoy big returns as children and grandchildren learn from the ones who have gone before them.

chapter 10
Maximizing
Cash

" Making money is easy. It is.
The difficult thing in life is not making it,
it's keeping it."

John McAfee

We've talked a lot about developing the Legacy Dimensions—Intellectual and Foundational—so you can add abundance in these areas to your family's Legacy Bank. You may be thinking, "Doug, I like all of that. We definitely need to focus on it all. But along with that, what about the money? What can I do to ensure my posterity can benefit from the Financial Dimension, as well?"

Let me start by telling you a story.

I grew up in a modest home. My father was bright, a hard worker; my parents were stellar role models; life was abundant, but money wasn't so much. I worked from the time I was fifteen, with my first steady job at Kentucky Fried Chicken. Sharee and I supported ourselves in college—she at a bookstore and me, at KFC. In my twenties, I began my career in insurance and securities, building my clientele door to door, relationship to relationship, studying the intricacies of the financial services industry as I went. By the time we were married just four years, things were already going well.

I had more financial ease than I had all my years growing up. In fact, Sharee and I were excited to be building our "dream home" in central Utah. It was 6,400 square feet, with a cathedral-beam, wood-decked ceilings, and a master bedroom deck where we could watch the deer and elk bed down in the scrub oak below. We thought we had the world by the tail! Two years later, in 1980, a bad recession hit America, and us.

We experienced unexpected, major setbacks due to a dishonest supervisor in the company I was working for. While the supervisor was being audited, my earnings (and that of two other producers) accumulated and were held in an escrow for nearly a year. As a result, we all found ourselves without an income, which meant Sharee and I got behind on our mortgage payments. Fortunately, we owned a rental duplex which we sold, and used the equity to bring the delinquent mortgage current.

But we got behind again. We owned a timeshare at a ski resort that we sold for triple what we had paid for it and were able to bring the mortgage current a second time. When we fell behind a third time, we realized we had no other liquid assets. With no light at the end of the tunnel in the foreseeable future, we decided to sell our house.

We listed our home for sale for $295,000, because it had appraised four years earlier for $305,000. No takers. (When supply is greater than demand, real estate values plummet.) We quickly lowered the price several times to $285,000, $275,000, $265,000; then down to $225,000 and even $195,000; but to no avail. We will never forget the day we went to the county courthouse in Provo, Utah, and on the steps at the sheriff's auction, we watched our beautiful home auctioned off in foreclosure proceedings. The other two producers that had their income put on hold also lost their homes in foreclosure.

Fortunately, Sharee and I were able to buy another home immediately thereafter with no money down—even with a foreclosure on our re-cord—because of a process I developed call The Negative Experi-ence Transformer, a method for turning any negative experience it into a positive learning opportunity that can bring about a better future. Since that negative experience, I have maintained liquidity on my real estate equity by keeping it safely separated from the property, which has enabled me to sail through several more recessions without losing real estate equity, even when the property dropped in value.

The experience of losing a house in foreclosure was a defining mo-ment for me as a financial strategist and retirement planning specialist. The results of this defining moment?

- I no longer took all financial advice for fact, and you shouldn't either.

- I learned to never follow the herd with regard to my money, and to pay little attention to the mainstream media (because they're part of the herd).

- I discovered the three key elements of all prudent investments or sensible financial instruments are: 1) liquidity (the ability to access your money when you need it), 2) safety of principal, and 3) rate of return. Real estate equity failed all three.

This experience was the genesis for developing the proven Live Abun-dant strategies that have since gone on to benefit thousands of lives across the country. As I alluded to in Chapter 3, these strategies have made it possible for people I teach to keep their financial assets po-sitioned with liquid access, safe, and earning predictable, tax-favored rates of return, so that no matter what has happened in the stock mar-ket or real estate market, they haven't lost a single penny of their prin-cipal due to market volatility—even during the Lost Decade of 2000 to 2010.

The reality is, the financial storms didn't end with the Lost Decade. With worldwide economic and political instability, domestic out-of-control spending, and more recessions in the forecast, there's every reason for Americans to be vigilant about maximizing their cash if they want it to go on to bless future generations.

So I share the story of losing our dream home for a reason. I experienced first-hand what it's like to lose what you've worked so hard to gain, due to external economic volatility. It's a wake-up call. Americans can't keep doing the same-old thing—putting money in traditional accounts like IRAs and 401(k)s in the market, hoping it will produce safe, liquid, tax-advantaged abundance for their retirement, and then for their children and grandchildren when they pass on.

It takes smarter thinking, better planning. And there's no better time than the present to get started.

THE LASER SOLUTION

I am a big proponent of everyone taking the time to educate themselves on different options for pursuing abundance in the Financial Dimension. There are many financial vehicles available, so it's important to find the ones that are the best fit for you.

With that in mind, I'll share here a brief overview of a solution that may be worth exploring as part of your approach to adding to your Financial Dimension. It's based on the three marvels of wealth accumulation, which are: 1) compound interest, 2) tax-favored accumulation, and 3) safe, positive leverage—the ability to own and control assets with very little or none of your money tied up or at risk in the asset. Personal financial disasters usually occur when one is highly leveraged with very little liquidity.

Now, the principle of leverage isn't bad in and of itself—actually it is the very essence of how money works. Safe leverage has created untold amounts of wealth in the world where a "win-win" is created again and again. When institutions like banks or credit unions borrow OPM (Other People's Money) and pay a low interest rate to people who "lend" it to them (when they deposit their money into the bank for savings), the banking institution then turns around and loans that money at higher interest rates to earn a net spread.

Earning interest is a win for the saver, while paying interest to the saver is a win for the bank, because they then loan out the same money at a higher rate. If a bank pays 1%, 2% or 3% interest on savings accounts, they turn around and loan that money at 5%, 6%, or higher. On just $1 million they may pay only $10,000 to $20,000 of annual interest (at 1% or 2%), but they are earning $50,000, $60,000 or more of interest (at 5%, 6% or more).

As a business owner, would you be willing to hire an employee for $20,000 if the employee made you an extra $60,000? Would you buy a widget machine for $20,000 if the machine made you an extra $60,000? That would be a 300% return on employment or equipment costs!

So leverage isn't bad; but leveraging without liquidity is what gets people into trouble. This wisdom motivated me to help people protect themselves from the negative impact of TIME, which is an acronym I use for:

- **T**axes
- **I**nflation
- **M**arket volatility
- **E**conomic uncertainty

One accomplishes this by maintaining LASER focus. LASER is another acronym that I came up with years ago that means:

- **L**iquid
- **A**ssets
- **S**afely
- **E**arning
- **R**eturns

All of the "serious cash" that I have earmarked for financially funding my Legacy Bank in perpetuity must meet the LASER test. As mentioned earlier, the three key elements of a prudent investment or any sensible financial instrument are:

1) **Liquidity**—This is the ability to access your money with a phone call or an electronic funds transfer (without triggering tax or a penalty).

2) **Safety of Principal**—This is the ability to preserve your principal and protect it from loss. Also, any year that you make money, you want to be able to lock in the gain and have it become newly protected principal so that you don't lose what you made in previous years due to market downturns.

3) **Rate of Return**—You want to be able to earn a competitive rate of return (tax-free) that historically has beaten inflation, because it is linked to the goods and services that inflate.

As an additional benefit, I prefer that the financial vehicles that meet the LASER test also have tax-advantages.

FEWER TAXES = MORE CASH IN THE LEGACY BANK

Whenever I speak and ask the audience, "Who thinks taxes will be going down in the future?" I get nothing but crickets. When I ask their opinion about the likelihood of tax increases, a sea of hands goes up.

Some estimates say taxes will likely go above 50% for many Americans in the future, and I wouldn't be surprised. America is addicted to spending—from programs like Social Security and Medicare to healthcare and countless other initiatives, Uncle Sam's appetite will only get bigger.

With taxes on the rise, I look for every valid and legal way to maximize my income and minimize my taxes. I'd rather redirect my money for causes I support that can truly make a difference for my country, as well as my family, than give that cash to the government in unnecessary taxes (that won't necessarily benefit the greatest national needs).

You may be thinking, "Well, that's true, but I won't have to worry about it too much in retirement. I'll be in a lower tax bracket then." What you also may not realize is when you reach retirement, you may lose many of the deductions you once enjoyed such as home mortgage interest, dependents, and retirement plan contributions. And if you're a business owner, you'll be losing even more deductions. It's what I call the Deduction Reduction, and it means that although you may have less income during retirement, your taxable income may be just as high or higher!

If you don't take action to avoid paying excess tax, you'll most likely be in for a rather unwelcomed surprise during your retirement years, which could result in living a lower lifestyle or outliving your money—which means no financial legacy for the family.

The key to minimizing taxes is to take ownership—being responsible and accountable—for your own future. Taxes are actually an asset. They pay for critical public services like police protection, public infrastructure, public education and so forth. But the secret to American wealth has always been in ownership—deeds, titles and articles of incorporation. When people take ownership (have skin in the game), they take better care of things. When was the last time you ever washed a rental car? People don't wash rental cars—they wash their own car!

When people don't take ownership for things like their retirement or health, the government tends to try to do it for them. But really, the government is pretty lousy at it. The US government currently owes about $130 trillion in future Social Security and Medicare benefits. It owes that money to Americans it has deducted premiums from, but the problem is, the government doesn't have that money in its coffers; it's gone. Social Security and Medicare are totally dependent on current and upcoming workers paying for debt incurred in the past.

The government realizes this is a problem—that's why it has decided to make some financial vehicles tax-favored. Uncle Sam understands that if people take responsibility for their own retirement or health, they are taking pressure off the government. Hence, you can take ownership and redirect otherwise payable taxes to your family bank that will help out the great country of America even more than just surrendering and paying more than necessary in tax. The idea is to be self-reliant vs. government-reliant; independent vs. dependent; to have skin in the game vs. getting something for nothing.

No matter how you look at it, paying less in taxes means having more for yourself and your future generations.

A NOT-SO-LITTLE SECRET

There's a secret the wealthy and privileged have known for decades, both personally and in their businesses: insurance, stuffed with cash to the limit allowed by the Internal Revenue Service, has incredible benefits. It protects portions of their assets and portfolios from the whims of economic ups and downs.

Take a guess where the major banks and Fortune 500 companies invest a lot of their tier-one assets (assets that they want absolutely safe and liquid). It's invested in BOLI and COLI (Bank-Owned Life Insurance and Corporate-Owned Life Insurance). Yep, banks have been earning—on the most conservative choices—3% to 5% tax-free on billions of dollars of OPM (other people's money)—and then they only pay 1% on that money people have in savings with them.

You can "by-pass the middle-man" with your serious cash. I'll use a little analogy from the children's story of The Three Little Pigs to explain. If you remember, the story details three little pigs being hunted by a wolf who blows the houses of straw and sticks down, but not the house of bricks. The straw house is like stock market values, which get blown away when the hurricanes of volatility rage. The house of sticks is like real estate, which is a little stronger and more predictable but also still shaky in economic turmoil. There are ways to minimize real estate risk, but that is a topic for another day.

There's a financial vehicle—something I call The LASER Fund because it provides **L**iquidity, **S**afety and predictable **R**ates of return—that when properly structured, is a house of bricks that can protect you from the storms of market volatility. It's a max-funded, tax-advantaged insurance contract, and it makes a great home for a portion of your serious retirement cash. Here is why:

- **Indexing** - Your money is linked to the market through indexing so that when the stock market performs well, you participate in the market gains. At the same time, if the market loses, your money is protected with a guaranteed floor.

- **Upside Potential** - Your cash value will receive an indexing credit, based on the market/index that you select. When that market grows during a segment, which is commonly twelve months, your cash value will be credited with interest. If the market gains 12%, you'll gain 12%. The upside potential is generally capped at rates from 12-16%.

- **Downside Protection** - If the market you are tied to has large losses, like in 2003 and 2008, your cash value won't decrease due to market performance. The downside risk is eliminated because of a guaranteed floor. Because your money is in your insurance policy and not in the market, and because of the guaranteed floor, it is safe and secure.

- **Lock and Reset** - Any gains—either from interest credited from an index or cash value due to excess premiums—are locked in and protected against loss, even if the index you are tied to loses. Each and every year this resets so gains are added to the principal and never lost due to market performance.

- **Liquidity** - Your policy cash value can be accessed tax-free. If you were to lose your job and need temporary income, your money is accessible.

In addition to protection from market volatility, have you ever seen an insurance policy that does the following?

1) Has cash value that equals or exceeds the premiums paid into it during the initial years?

2) Has an internal rate of return averaging in excess of 7%—thereby doubling your money about every ten years?

3) Allows you to access your money at a 7% to 10% payout rate without depleting your principal?

4) The insurance can get cheaper as you get older?

When The LASER Fund is structured correctly and funded properly, it can do all of the above and a whole lot more. Many highly successful people use it as a working capital account for real estate portfolios or operating a business—to act as their own banker.

THE EVOLUTION OF THE LASER FUND

For a deeper understanding, it's helpful trace the history behind the development of the LASER Fund. When I first started in the financial services industry in 1974, I was a big proponent of "buy term and invest the difference." I insured people with term insurance and invested their money in mutual funds of their choice. I had a Series 1 securities license. By 1980, I was responsible for more than 3,000 clients in thirteen western states. We were working hard to help people earn an average of

12% in the market. But it was like playing red-light, green-light as a kid.

During some periods of time, people would earn more than 20% (like taking twenty steps forward), only to then lose 10% (taking ten steps backward). But the real wake-up call was that even if a person could average 12% (a net of twelve steps forward), sooner or later, they would have to take at least four steps back, due to taxes they would end up paying. In other words, if you had a $1,000,000 nest egg at retirement in a tax-deferred IRA or 401(k)—even if you earned as high as 12% ($120,000)—most retirees had to pay at least one-third of that $120,000 (which is $40,000) in taxes between federal and state income tax. So they were only really earning a net of 8%.

On top of that, the financial advisor and broker-dealer were usually charging asset management fees of 0.5% to 1%. So a retiree was only really netting $70,000 to buy gas, groceries, prescriptions, golf green fees, etc. You may be saying to yourself, "Well, I can get by on $70,000 per year." What you may not realize is that at projected rates of inflation (due to irresponsible government spending and the printing of money), that $70,000 will be able to buy much less in ten years, and even less in fifteen, less in twenty, and so on.

To help people avoid outliving their money during retirement, the financial services industry came out with the "4% rule." With this rule, they recommend that people pull out no more than 4% from their retirement nest egg each year. (While this practice is meant to protect retirees from depleting their nest eggs, it's important to note that it may not be enough. Even the 4% rule has come into question within the last few years, with analyses showing that it may fail in preventing a good portion of retirees from outliving their money, due to market volatility and longer life expectancies.)

Following the 4% rule, what if a retiree, in addition to other sources of income (pension, Social Security, rental income), wanted to pull $3,000 a month out of her 401(k) to cover the extras (travel, medical, charitable giving)? That would be $36,000 a year. She would have to withdraw about $50,000 per year and pay taxes of $14,000, to end up with

$36,000 for her needs. That $50,000 represents 4% of $1,250,000. If you're like me, I don't want to work hard to save $1,250,000 to have a measly $3,000 a month of income!

Structured properly and funded correctly, a LASER Fund can possibly generate a 7% payout ($87,500 per year on a policy with a cash value of $1,250,000) tax-free, without exhausting the policy.

In 1980, many brokerage firms were recommending that investors buy the same stocks and bonds that insurance companies buy—because the multitrillion-dollar insurance industry has long been the backbone of not only America, but also the world. Legal reserve insurance companies have been much more conservative with their investments because they have to maintain the utmost liquidity and safety. Hence, during the Great Depression—even though thousands of banks went under, legal reserve insurance companies fared well. The same was true during the period of 2008 - 2012—more than 400 banks went under (with about 900 more on the watch list), while legal reserve insurance companies largely weathered the economic storm intact.

E.F. Hutton, a former well-known brokerage firm, is often credited for the emergence of max-funded, tax-advantaged insurance. The company simply posed the question: Why do we always have to expose people's money in the market—trying to achieve 10% - 12% taxable returns (only netting 7% - 8%)—when we can put the same money into an insurance policy and earn an average of 7% tax-advantaged, without all of the volatility and risk?

It was brilliant! It was the "buy term and invest the difference" concept protected under a tax-free umbrella. So instead of trying to get life insurance for the cheapest premium only for death benefit, Hutton flipped it to where people got the least amount of insurance possible to accommodate the most money that the IRS would allow—and as fast as the IRS would allow premiums to be paid—so as to not exceed the definition of a life insurance policy.

So I began transferring my clients' money from the market into max-funded insurance contracts, and they were never happier. In the 1980s, many retirees were paying $500,000 into an insurance contract and were able to take a 10% payout ($50,000) per year, tax-free, without depleting their principal.

The Internal Revenue Service was worried about all the money migrating away from traditional accounts and toward insurance, so it challenged this concept in 1982 and 1984. Through Congress, the IRS argued that life insurance contracts that were maximum-funded were not really insurance policies but, in fact "investments." They wanted to put parameters on the life insurance policies, which were passed as part of the Tax and Fiscal Responsibility Act of 1982 and also the Deficit Reduction Act of 1984. In the insurance industry, these two acts are commonly referred to as TEFRA and DEFRA.

The TEFRA and DEFRA citation, or tax corridor, basically dictates the minimum death benefit required in order to accommodate the ultimate desired aggregate premium basis, based on the insured's age, gender, and health. In other words, if a person wanted to use a cash-value life insurance policy for tax-advantaged capital accumulation purposes, TEFRA and DEFRA guidelines would dictate the amount of the minimum death benefit required without exceeding the definition of a life insurance contract. This will make the accumulation of cash values and the death benefit not subject to tax. Therefore, the following disclaimer must be made:

**Life insurance policies are not investments and,
accordingly, should not be purchased as an investment.**

In my opinion, these funds are way better than an "investment," because investments are usually subject to tax and market volatility. Rather, it's a "financial instrument" that is not a "qualified retirement plan;" you can "put" money into, and it can be used for tax-free income during your "golden years" that can be structured to provide:

- Extreme liquidity
- Tremendous safety
- Stable rates of return
- Tax-free income

Often I ask audiences what they would call something that you put money into that can grow safely at an average return of 7% tax-deferred, and that gives you tax-free access to your money—but it's NOT a "qualified retirement plan"? The overwhelming responses have included, "That would be a miracle, a dream solution."

On June 21, 1988, Congress passed the Technical and Miscellaneous Revenue Act (TAMRA) which had provisions where the banking and brokerage industries lobbied Congress to "slow the flow" of money out of their institutions to max-funded insurance contracts, because it was hard for them to compete with the benefits of said contracts. But they didn't want to take away the tax benefits altogether, because these contracts are where many of these institutions invest some of their own money, as well. (A little later in this chapter, I'll explain compliance with the TEFRA/DEFRA and TAMRA tax citations using an apartment building as a metaphor.)

BENEFITS FOR LIFE

You may be thinking now, "Wait, Doug. When most people think about insurance, they think about it strictly as a 'death benefit.' When the insured dies, this death benefit covers immediate needs such as income replacement, estate preservation, and mortgage/debt protection, right?"

And that's right, as I mentioned earlier if you only want your insurance to cover those needs, you'd want to insure yourself for the most amount of death benefit with the least amount of premium. The objective with The LASER Fund, however, is to structure your policy to have the least amount of death benefit with the maximum amount of cash in the policy as allowed by the IRS.

When you build a LASER Fund account, you would determine, with the assistance of a trained Wealth Architect, how much cash you can place into your contract. There is no limit to how much it can grow—only how much you can pay into it. Through a unique process, your Wealth Architect will then determine the minimum amount of insurance you'll need to be in full compliance with the IRS tax code. This ensures that money inside the contract, once it is in force, qualifies for tax-free access and to grow tax-deferred.

Now I'll share that apartment complex analogy to help you better understand The LASER Fund, how it is created, and then how you fund it.

This type of insurance policy can be compared to owning an apartment building. If you were to own your own five-story apartment building, the goal would be to rent out all five floors in order to maximize profit and minimize expenses. If only the first floor were rented out, and the remaining floors were left vacant, costs would remain extremely high and eat away your profits.

The LASER Fund is similar. To maximize your returns and minimize your expenses, you would fill up your contract with maximum planned premiums (this is like renting out all the available space). This can be accomplished in as few as five years to be compliant with TAMRA guidelines.

There are four distinct, yet equally important phases, when creating and funding your insurance contract.

Phase I - Design and Approval - Based on the individual's financial and retirement goals, the Wealth Architect helps determine the size of The LASER Fund contract. These contracts can be structured to hold thousands or even millions of dollars. They can be filled using only monthly or periodic payments, or they can accommodate large lump sum payments. They can also be funded using a combination of both.

Based on the financial objectives and assets available, the Wealth Architect designs the contract to comply with IRS guidelines to allow for tax-deferred growth and tax-free access. It is important to remember that Phase I is the planning and approval phase, and the realization of tax-deferred growth and tax-free access is achieved through Phases II, III, and IV.

The plan then gets submitted to select insurance companies for approval and underwriting. While in underwriting, the insurance company will look at the size of the insurance policy, the need for insurance, insurability, and a variety of other factors. (It may surprise you to know that people with previous medical conditions or people who may be older can get approved with excellent rates with some insurance companies.)

I can't stress enough the importance of working with financial profes-sionals who are experienced in coordinating max-funded contracts. A lack of experience can have dire consequences. Once an apartment is built, changes are difficult to make regarding structure and floor plans. Similarly, an insurance contract may be difficult to change, as well, without incurring significant expense, especially if it was structured incorrectly from the beginning. The process of proper and effective LASER Fund design is significant and necessary in order to maximize long-term benefits, minimize risks, and keep it flexible.

Be aware that not all insurance companies have the products that per-form well when structured this way. To be specific, out of the massive insurance industry in the United States, only a select few companies have the ratings and the products that have passed our high standard of scrutiny—less than a dozen, in fact.

Phase II - Acquisition - Once Phase I is complete and your in-surance contract has been designed and approved, the next stage begins when the individual puts it in force. This simply means that the first premium payment is made, paid directly into the accounts of the insurance company selected for the policy.

Once the money is received by the insurance company, the death ben-efit is in place in order to better protect your estate and assets. If an unforeseen tragedy were to occur, the premiums you would have paid into the policy would blossom into a much larger benefit for the family and loved ones or the estate.

Consider the entire first year the policy is owned to be Phase II. During this year, it's best to fill up the contract with all the planned premium payments. Near the end of the first year, also called the anniversary date, the individual receives an annual statement from the insurance company in the mail that details the amount of premium paid, cash value that has accumulated, and costs that have been charged during this year. An annual review is also held with the Wealth Architect.

Every insurance contract is different, but generally the minimum amount of time it takes to maximum fund an insurance policy is five years, according to IRS guidelines (TAMRA). In other words, the IRS doesn't let anyone put the entire amount of planned cash into the policy in one year—they make people spread it over a period of years, often five—otherwise when they go to access the money, it won't be totally tax-free.

At the end of Phase II, The LASER Fund is usually about one-fifth max-funded. If you only have one-fifth of your apartment building rented out, will the business of owning an apartment be profitable? Of course not. If only the first floor were rented out and the remaining floors were left vacant, costs would remain extremely high and would eat away your profits. Designing and funding The LASER Fund the first year is similar to the apartment building. It isn't profitable … yet. It needs to be max-funded over the next four years or more.

Phase III - Maximum Funding - The next phase in The LASER Fund is to fill the policy with all the planned premiums. This phase is generally Years 2 - 5 but can take longer, depending on the plan and whether it's funded according to that plan. We recommend that clients meet with Wealth Architects annually to set goals or make adjustments as necessary.

During Years 2 - 5, optimally the individual will continue to fill up the policy with all the planned premiums. It's a lot like when renting out more floors of the apartment—you have more rent payments coming in, offsetting the costs of running the apartment building. Similarly, when you're filling up your policy, your cash value is growing, giving you the opportunity to earn more interest—which can offset your fees. What's more, your cash value will not lose principal due to market volatility—even if the economy and stock market take a serious dive.

As the years progress, the cost of the insurance can go down as the individual gets older. This is because the amount of insurance at risk to the insurance company is reduced as it is replaced with the individual's money and the interest earnings on that money. The goal is to have only a small portion of the individual's interest that is earned paying for the insurance, which is required by the IRS for it to qualify as a tax-free contract—thus eventually earning a net tax-free rate of return that is very attractive.

One of the best parts of The LASER Fund? As the cash value begins to accumulate in your policy, these funds may be accessed at any time through a phone call to the insurance company. They will promptly put a check in the mail or do an electronic transfer. If an individual chooses to access from the policy in the first five years, he must keep in mind that policies perform best when they are maximum-funded. The best time to access money from the policy is after it is funded to the maximum amount allowed.

Filling the policy up to maximum levels is like finally renting out the entire apartment building. With your building completely leased out, it is now optimized for profits.

Phase IV - Profits and Distribution - Phase IV is like having the building fully rented, and with The LASER Fund maximum-funded, the individual can work with the Wealth Architect to decide when to take out money, how often, and how much to access from the cash value on a tax-free basis. The policy can continue to grow through the miracle of compound interest. Based on the index it is linked to, the contract will be credited with interest earned.

One of the nice benefits of these kinds of policies? When they are max-funded, they can become very inexpensive in Phase IV, due to the large amounts of cash in the policy. Let's say someone has had her policy in force for ten years, the policy has a death benefit of $1,000,000, and it has accumulated a cash value of $800,000. She's only going to pay costs to cover the remaining $200,000 of insurance that is at risk to the insurance company—the remainder is now her own money. If the insured were to pass away, the beneficiary would receive a total amount of $1,000,000 in tax-free death benefit.

This is by far the most superior way to accomplish what the "buy term and invest the difference" proponents say, because individuals are actually becoming self-insured—but this way it's totally tax free, and it's faster and performs much better.

The best way to access money from the account is through tax-free loans, as I'll explain in the next section. As long as the policy remains in force, no tax will be owed on these loans. If, however, an individual were to surrender the policy and cancel it, that may create a taxable event. That would not be smartest exit strategy, but nonetheless, any cash put directly into the policy (basis), would remain tax-free, as it has already been taxed.

THE LASER FUND'S TAX ADVANTAGES

In my opinion, as part of your tax-reducing retirement strategy you should look seriously at The LASER Fund Solution. As important as the death benefit, these contracts can be structured to hold your serious cash (by serious cash I mean money you have set aside for long-term goals like retirement).

When structured correctly and then funded properly, these contracts shelter you from the danger of increased taxation. To be clear, the tax advantages of these contracts are no secret or shadow game, just simply too complex for the average financial advisor or financial professional to implement without developing an expertise through years of research and training. Unfortunately, many advisors or accountants who "haven't done their research" end up having strong and uneducated opinions that are not based on facts, especially regarding the tax benefits and internal rate of return that can be achieved.

Sometimes, I've heard mainstream financial advisors retort, "Well, I've never seen an insurance policy perform like that!" So they assume they don't exist. When that is the basis for their reasoning, it would be fair to ask, "Well, have you ever seen your brain? How do you know that exists?" The fact is, I've witnessed countless insurance contracts that were structured correctly and funded properly that have had net, internal rates of return averaging 7% - 10% tax-free on all premiums paid into the policy. Many people have experienced tax-free payout rates of 7% - 10% annually from their insurance policies without depleting principal.

Here is how a properly structured contract can shelter you from increased taxation:

Tax Savings #1 - Money put into these insurance contracts has already been taxed at today's rates, not tomorrow's. With tax rates likely going up in the future to unknown amounts, getting taxes over and done is incredibly important and financially significant. Always paying taxes on the seed money rather than the money you harvest is sound advice.

Tax Savings #2 - Money taken out of your contract, when done in accordance with Internal Revenue Code guidelines is not regarded as taxable income, as opposed to income from a traditional IRA/401(k). For more than one hundred years the money that accumulates inside of a life insurance policy does so tax-favored. You can also access your money tax-free from a max-funded, tax-advantaged insurance contract via a loan, rather than a withdrawal. Here's why:

When done correctly, it is a loan made to yourself that is never due or payable in your lifetime. To be in compliance with IRS guidelines, an interest rate is typically charged. Then that interest is offset with interest that is credited on the money you didn't "withdraw" but rather, remained there as collateral for your loan, thus resulting in a zero net cost in many instances.

Many times, rather than just a zero net cost, I have chosen an "indexed loan" or "participating loan," which means that the money in the insurance policy continued to earn the indexed rate (which historically averaged 7% - 10% tax-deferred), while the insurance company was charging interest on my loan (as required to keep the cash flow tax-free under the IRS code) at a fixed rate of only 5%. This strategy often allows you to take out a higher tax-free income because you are borrowing at a lower rate (in my case in this example, at 5%), and your money stays in the policy, earning at a higher rate (in my example, 7% to 10%).

Loans taken from your contract ARE NOT TAXED because they aren't deemed earned, passive, or portfolio income—which are the only types of income (since the 1986 Tax Reform Act) that are subject to income tax on a 1040 tax return. See section 7702 of the Internal Revenue Code.

Although the insurance company does not require you to pay back any loans during your lifetime (because any loan balances are washed away when the death benefit is ultimately paid), you can pay back some or all of the loan if you choose. In essence, any loan repayment is actually new cash put into policy and simply allows tax-free interest on "new money" placed into a policy—even though it may have been once "maxed out." This is a brilliant strategy used by people who want to use the insurance contract like I do as a working capital account in their Legacy Bank.

Tax Savings #3 - As a "life insurance policy" increases in value due to competitive interest being earned, no taxes are due on that gain, as long as the policy remains in force. Many financial instruments, such as savings accounts, CDs, mutual funds, and money markets will typically have tax liability on their gain. *See section 72(e) of the Internal Revenue Code.*

Tax Savings #4 - Upon your death, the money in your insurance policy transfers to your heirs and beneficiaries completely income tax-free. *See section 101(a) of the Internal Revenue Code.*

Policy loans and withdrawals will reduce available cash values and death benefits and may cause the policy to lapse, or affect guarantees against lapse. Additional premium payments may be required to keep the policy in force. In the event of a lapse, outstanding policy loans in excess of unrecovered cost basis will be subject to ordinary income tax. Tax laws are subject to change and you should consult a tax professional.

Policy loans are not usually subject to income tax unless the policy is classified as a modified endowment contract (MEC) under IRC Section 7702A. However, withdrawals or partial surrenders from a non-MEC policy are subject to income tax to the extent that the amount distributed exceeds the owner's cost basis in the policy.

In summary, in the four decades that I have been a financial strategist, I have never seen any other vehicle that accumulates money totally tax-favored, then later allows you to access your money totally tax-free. Then when you ultimately pass away, it blossoms (increases) in value and transfers to your heirs totally income-tax free.

As a side note, I don't recommend that every dollar you set aside be in The LASER Fund. Just know that huge amounts of taxes can be reduced by including this type of insurance contract in your retirement portfolio—or by making it your primary retirement planning strategy like me and thousands of other highly-successful, wealthy people.

Now I very well know that you may be thinking, "I've always thought that insurance, in general, was a poor investment." Actually, I agree … because it's not an "investment!" It's an insurance policy, and unfortunately most insurance is not structured correctly nor funded properly to accomplish these results. Here are the mistakes I often see that are made by advisors who don't understand it completely and/or people who don't follow through:

- It's not structured properly under TEFRA, DEFRA guidelines
- It's not funded correctly
- It's not designed in accordance with IRS guidelines to be tax-free under TAMRA, Sec. 72(e), 7702, and 101(a)
- The wrong product was used
- The wrong company was chosen
- The advisor was not proficient

WHY WOULDN'T YOU GENERATE MORE WEALTH?

To demonstrate how powerful this strategy can be for your family Legacy Bank, I'll share an example using a metaphor. I have observed that many financial advisors focus on commodities: buy this mutual fund; buy this stock; buy gold or silver. It's not in the commodity—it's in the strategy. Many financial planners try to "charge up a retirement battery" with hopefully enough "juice" so it won't go dead before the retirees do. The things that cause people's retirement batteries to short out are: 1) taxes, 2) inflation, and 3) market volatility. The essence of this book and this chapter is to have you consider a powerful generator to power all Three Dimensions of your Authentic Wealth—not just your money. Then it can truly become "generational wealth" that goes on in perpetuity.

I often ask my audiences, "Why would you generate 4%, when you could safely generate an average of 7%? Why would you leave behind to your family (or favorite charities) X, when you could leave behind double or triple X—tax-free? In other words, on an account with $1 million in it, why would you settle for $40,000 a year of payout when you could generate $70,000 of annual payout tax-free? Why would you leave behind $1 million taxable, when you could leave even more, tax-free?"

Here's a story to illustrate: a wonderful gentleman came to Live Abundant a few years ago and attended our Abundance by Choice educational sessions. His wife had just passed away. He was seventy years old. He had $600,000 in his IRAs and 401(k)s, among several other assets, including real estate. After getting enlightened about opportunities that he didn't know existed before, he went through our unique eight-step True Wealth Transformation process to set up his Legacy Bank and reposition many of his financial assets to optimize his liquidity, safety, and rate of return. He also wanted to minimize the taxes he was paying.

His previous advisor had insisted that he take only 4% per year (the 4% rule) from his IRAs and 401(k)s, or the RMD (Required Minimum Distribution) to stretch out the tax liability for the rest of his life and transfer his IRAs and 401(k)s to his children.

Now 4% on $600,000 was $24,000 per year. He would have owed at least one-third of that in taxes ($8,000 a year), netting him only $16,000 per year to enjoy for his retirement! Not only that, under that scenario, when he ultimately passed away, the $600,000 was going to be whittled down by at least 40% - 50% with income taxes and possibly some estate taxes as it passed to his heirs.

In a nutshell, with our assistance, he performed a strategic roll-out (not a roll-over), from his IRAs and 401(k)s over a five-year period using a structured payout vehicle, where he locked in an 8.25% effective yield on his IRAs and 401(k)s. He transferred approximately $12,500 per month ($150,000) per year out of his IRAs and 401(k)s and got the taxes over and done with rather than "stretching the taxes out"— which usually ends up with far more taxes paid by continuing to defer. (To me, deferred taxes simply means increased taxes).

With tax planning strategies, he was able to offset a large portion of the taxes on his IRAs and 401(k)s with new deductions we helped him create—primarily on his real estate holdings. At the end of the five-year roll-out period, he successfully had transferred a grand total of $750,000 into his LASER Fund insurance contracts. He has been experiencing an average of more than 8% net annual return on his insurance contracts, and with rebalancing his portfolio every twelve to twenty-four months, he is approaching closer to a 10% average return.

To summarize, he has now experienced $60,000 - $75,000 per year of tax-free cash flow (8% - 10% payout on $750,000). That is close to quadruple what he was destined to settle for under the "battery approach." Now he can "generate" far more to bless his life and his family. He can establish his rules of governance to provide equal opportunities through his family's Legacy Bank to help his posterity with loans, grants, and scholarships. These opportunities can be aligned with his and his deceased wife's True Wealth Philosophy. If his children or grandchildren want to utilize their equal opportunities today, they can turn to Grandpa rather than applying for a loan with a commercial bank. He can access the money instantly in his insurance contracts—which is much easier for his family than having to go through the lengthy process of loan qualifications with the bank. As his children pay back their loans to his Legacy Bank—he simply pays the loan back to his LASER Fund insurance policy, which can then be used for future family needs.

The best part is, his Legacy Bank is set up just like mine. When he ultimately passes away (because none of us is getting out of here alive—I mean in this life—we're all going to die), whatever money is left in his LASER Fund instantly blossoms tax-free. In his case, he would likely leave behind $1.2 million or more, tax-free, instead of the $600,000 yet-to-be-taxed IRAs and 401(k)s.

You see, in my family Legacy Bank, we use The LASER Fund (max-funded insurance contracts) as our primary vehicle, because when the patriarch and matriarch passes on, the Legacy Bank receives a tremendous infusion of tax-free cash to keep our family bank funded at a growth rate equal to or greater than our posterity grows. We have a rule of governance that dictates that the tax-free proceeds paid from the insurance contracts at death are to fund new tax-free insurance contracts on the lives of the oldest family members in the next generation. Hence we have financially created "generational wealth."

Are you getting it? You see, this chapter isn't in this book to promote insurance. If used properly like explained herein, I'm convinced it is the strongest financial instrument to effectively fund your Legacy Bank in perpetuity as the money keeps blossoming.

THE END-GAME

Whatever financial vehicles you choose, ultimately the goal is the same: optimizing abundance in your Financial Dimension. Financial abundance can fuel so many meaningful endeavors—from helping support your children in achieving an education, to philanthropic service, to weddings, to business ventures, to emergency or medical needs, and more. It can help provide for things like Family Retreats with a Purpose, second homes, etc.

Of course, all of this can and should be managed in a way that empowers your children rather than entitles them, through a sound KASH Blueprint that outlines your rules of governance for borrowing from the family's Legacy Bank. Combining your KASH Blueprint with your family's visions and values can create a bonding, unified effort, a sense of teamwork that lasts for generations. Your posterity can then thrive in the Abundance Cycle rather than the Entitlement Cycle, which can lead to lasting Authentic Wealth.

chapter 11
Entitlement
in the Workplace

" Always deliver more than expected."

Larry Page

.

There are times at Live Abundant when it's all hands on deck. We may have three or four seminars in a given week, spread across several states. We have stacks of booklets to coordinate; audio visual equipment to ship; flights and lodging to arrange; follow-up with attendees to manage; and the day-to-day client service to attend to. This often requires the entire staff to jump in, help out, and sometimes even step beyond the scope of their regular roles.

I've been fortunate to be surrounded by success-minded people throughout my forty-plus years running a company, the kind of people who are focused on the end goal—our clients' abundance—and who are willing to do what it takes when things are busy. However, I do re-call a time when one of our staff members would constantly grumble, "That's not in my job description."

I'm not a fan of entitlement at home—and I find it equally appalling in the workplace. Entitlement at work has become a major problem for companies across America. Too many businesses when asked, "How many employees do you have working for you?" could respond, "Oh about half of them!"

I have several clients who run businesses, and they often ask me what they can do to prevent entitlement from destroying their companies. They bring me in to speak to their workforce, to talk about taking re-sponsibility and accountability, to help them initiate the $2 Rule, and to discuss having an abundance mindset.

In this chapter I'll extend the scope from entitlement within families to entitlement in the workplace—and discuss what you can do about it.

DIAGNOSING THE PROBLEM

Just like a disease, entitlement has several symptoms, and it's impor-tant to notice the signs. It can appear in laziness, wanting something for nothing, cheating the system, and more.

For example, I had an assistant once who was habitually fifteen to twenty minutes late. I finally had a heart-to-heart talk with her, and I said, "You know what? I've been prepared to give you a raise, but if you remember when I hired you, I said there were four things that will matter: be on time, finish what you start, do what you say you're going to do, and remember to say please and thank you.* You're pretty good at three of them, but being on time …"

She shrugged her shoulders and said, "I've just never been on time in my life. I'm always late. I've worked here a long time. Isn't that enough for a raise?" I replied, "Well, those were the four criteria that I hired you

---

* These four habits comprise The Referability Factor™, Strategic Coach Dan Sullivan's standards for earning respect and future referrals.

on, right? I'll tell you what. Instead of a raise, let's try looking at it as a bonus. If you can be here ten minutes early next month—how about just eighteen of the twenty-two work days—I'll give you a $300 bonus."

She was early every day—until she received the bonus. Unfortunately after that she went right back to being late. A few weeks later she asked about that raise, and I reminded her she had gone back to being late. She was frustrated—but I held firm, accountability mattered. She ended up taking another job for a while, but came back because she missed our environment and camaraderie. Since I believe in second chances, I gave her similar incentives for productive results, which she met, and she stayed with us several more years. Through her I learned it helps to be clear and reward performance.

On the other hand, sometimes clarity doesn't seem to matter. We had a staff member once who would help himself to the snacks and sodas we stock for client events. Now, a drink or a pack of nuts here and there is actually encouraged at our office. But it's not our policy for employees to go "free shopping" through the inventory, and this gentleman was loading his briefcase every day, taking piles of snacks home to his family.

Then when we were booking a big seminar event at a hotel, he called Marriott separately to ask if they could transfer all of the award points from the company account to his personal account. When I asked him about it, his attitude was, ""Well, you guys don't pay me enough, and I deserve some perks, so I went ahead and created my own." Needless to say he didn't last much longer with us.

Sometimes people are clock watchers—they just show up and do the bare minimum until it's time to go home. At one time I owned a manufacturing company, and we put in a time clock. My son-in-law was our supervisor, and he started noticing people would run in, punch their timesheets, then go back out to their car, or get on their phones. They would waste twenty or thirty minutes before actually getting to work. Soon other employees decided they'd join in the clock-punching antics. They'd even call co-workers and ask them to punch in for them if they were going to be late.

We see this in a lot of environments where there's a system set up to keep people honest, but then employees try to cheat that system. We get "circumventers." How different would it be if instead employees were self-motivated? What if they came with "batteries included?"

This all goes back to that scarcity versus abundance mindset. It manifests itself in the way people talk, the way they act, and the way that competition arises. Employees think they're competing in every meeting and even every conversation at the water cooler. Segregation enters in: they see the company as employees versus management, department versus department, hourly workers versus salaried.

Employees start to gripe among themselves, "Management doesn't do anything. We're the ones who do all the work. The owners are lazy and greedy!" Or they'll say things like, "That's not my job—you're going to pay me more since you asked me to do that additional task, right?" Or "I'm the bookkeeper—not the janitor!" (This one makes me chuckle, as I've always been quick to help clean up the leftover plates and napkins or grab the vacuum after our events.)

Entitlement is also evident when employees are more focused on their "right" to have a vast amount of sick days, vacation days and personal days, rather than looking at what they can contribute on all the days they're in the office. I think it's important for employees to realize they're either a cost, a liability to your company, or they're an asset. You are investing in them. It's likely the assets will be kept around much longer than the liabilities.

Of course not all employees are like this, but it seems to mirror our nation, where it's almost a 50/50 ratio of citizens who want to take versus give. The takers, the tax-eaters, have the mentality, "How much can I take? How much can I get? Can I get more than I contributed?" That kind of outlook stands in stark contrast to what John F. Kennedy said,

"Ask not what your country can do for you, ask what you can do for your country." President Kennedy saw the need to caution Americans against becoming a nation of pilferers versus contributors.

This negative, me-me-me entitlement mentality can become a cancer in the workplace. One of the brokers I work with described that at his office, he and his team decided to avoid the company's daily doughnut break. It's not that they were against enjoying a treat—it's that the breakroom had become a cesspool of negativity, competition, complaining, and backstabbing. His team, instead, decided to gather together and focus on positivity and productivity.

So if all this entitlement threatens to take a company off course, what can we do to get the employees back on track, collaborating in an environment of abundance? There are a few key strategies—and it starts with the culture that you create, from the top down.

CULTURE MATTERS

When I've worked with company leaders, I've shared this analogy to help them understand the importance of the abundance mindset, and to give them a framework to begin the discussion with their employees.

I ask them, "Are you a fountain or a drain?"

I then share that I recently spent time touring Italy. It probably wasn't the typical American's trip—mine was on the back of a Harley Davidson with Sharee, surrounded by a group of dentists, doctors, and other professionals who were also Harley riders. We were there to take in the history and culture, share professional insights, and raise money for the nonprofit Learning Curves, which my brother-in-law, Dr. Roy Hammond, founded to support Smiles for Hope, a nonprofit that delivers dental and medical care and supplies to third-world communities in need.

While traveling through Tuscany, I was impressed with the scenery (stunning landscapes, sweeping hills), the people (warm, open, full of life), and the timelessness of it all. I was also intrigued by the fountains. One of the area's most famous fountains, Fontebranda, has three basins at different heights—the first for drinking water, the second for people to bring their animals to drink, and the third to wash clothes and tend to other daily needs. Another notable fountain, Fonte Gaia, was named in honor of the joy the citizens felt when water first arrived in the town square in the mid-1300s.

But even more awe-inspiring than the Siena fountains' architecture is the actual fountain mechanics. During the Middle Ages, the Tuscans built a complicated system of underground tunnels and hydraulics to bring water from deep below the hillside city up to the surface.

We're not much different from these fountains. Water didn't magically appear in them. It took an immense amount of ingenuity and effort for the Tuscans to build the network of tunnels, as well as artistry to design the masterpieces that adorned them. Just the same, a productive, abundant life doesn't "just happen" for us. It requires focused, consistent effort to develop skills, knowledge, and abilities. And the more selective and determined we are with the way we spend our time, talents, resources, and energy—and in the company we keep—the more likely we are to "flow" with abundance.

It's not unlike when Sharee and I were raising our six children. We often told them it's great to be friendly with a lot of people, but be very careful whom you are friends with. Because whether we like to admit it or not, who we become ten, twenty, or thirty years from now is the product of what we bring into our lives. What we feed our hearts with (spirituality, friends, family, associates, etc.), what we feed our brains with (books, music, social media), what we feed our bodies with (food, liquid, nutrients) impact who we become spiritually, mentally, and physically. In other words, what we take in goes into our waterways. Are we gathering waste water and rubbish along the way, or are we flowing with pure, clear water from pristine, natural sources?

I've been part of a group of the nation's leading thinkers and professionals, called the Genius Network Mastermind, for quite some time. When we meet, it's to share some of the best thinking, the most successful strategies we've each garnered in our different fields. Many of these ideas have helped shape the philosophies and strategies that we've all incorporated in our businesses and lives over the years.

As an author and speaker, I've also been able to share the top ideas in my books and presentations. I love seeing the lightbulbs go on, the "aha" moments happening in real-time, as I talk to different audiences. And here's why: truly sound, proven ideas provide clarity, confidence, and the opportunity to develop even greater capability. It's like "pure water" that I've been able to "bring up through the tunnels" and share at the public fountain.

This is where it's important to ask yourself (and encourage employees to do the same): what kind of fountain do you want to be? Then you need to look at clearing out any negative habits that might be holding you back, causing you to leak water, or worse, become an absolute drain. As you do, you'll be on your way to a more abundant work life—continually springing forth with ideas, energy, and success that will go on to elevate the company, as well.

HEALTHY COMPETITION

You can also encourage your employees to foster a sense of healthy competition and camaraderie.

At some of the large manufacturing companies during the Industrial Revolution, back when the unions came in, many saw a shift in company culture. All of a sudden the mentality became, "Don't produce any more than the minimum during your shift, because you'll make the rest of us look bad."

A story is told that one day, one of the workers at a factory decided to change things. He came in and drew a great big number "9" in chalk on the floor where they were putting together their parts for the finished product.

The next shift came in and asked what it was for. He explained, "That's how many parts we put out during our shift. I know we've been just doing eight for a long time, but our shift, we've got the best people, and we put out nine." The next shift smelled competition in the air. They put out ten. They erased the nine and drew a big ten on the floor.

The following shift asked about it, and they raised the bar to eleven.

The company was able to double productivity within three weeks, just because everybody started taking pride in being more productive.

ENCOURAGE INGENUITY

With our growing client base in forty-seven of fifty states, my team and I were running to keep up with the demands of booking travel and coordinating equipment and supplies for people going in several directions at once. I had a staff member who noticed the chaos, and jumped in, saying, "We're having major issues with travel. I think I can solve it."

She took it on, developing spreadsheets and communicating with the team. Suddenly our travel logistics went from bumpy to smooth. She was proactive. She took ownership of a problem, and we recognized her efforts in front of the entire team. Her example helped ignite a contagious can-do attitude that other employees mirrored. And not surprisingly, when we needed to promote a supervisor, we knew right where to look—someone who used her own ingenuity and took the initiative to make the entire company more successful.

Julian Simon taught there is only one natural resource on the planet— human ingenuity. If you think about it, oil was just something that got camels' hooves dirty until someone figured out how to make combustible engines.

So invite your employees to add their ingenuity to the company. You might be amazed at the impact it can have—and how it will help curb entitlement.

HIRE RIGHT

While shifting the company culture is important, it's also critical to hire the right kind of people from the get-go. There may be different skill sets you're looking for to fill different positions, and there are likely common qualities that you want across the board.

For me, three things matter most when I'm interviewing. I look for:

1. Someone who is a fit for our culture
2. Talent, or Unique Ability®
3. Experience

Sometimes business leaders have been surprised that experience is third on my list. But I have found anyone can gain the experience needed—if I don't have someone who has innate talent or who isn't going to fit within our environment, all the experience in the world won't compensate. Whenever I have given in and hired someone that really didn't fit our abundance mindset and TEAM culture where "Together Everyone Achieves More," the "misfit" has been miserable and we have regretted it.

It's awkward—for everyone. They usually voluntarily leave before being converted because they realize no one else in the company is buying into a scarcity mindset with all the accompanying backstabbing, gossiping, blaming, justifying, and jockeying for position. Sometimes, they administer some poisonous attitudes, but it can be remedied if done quickly and confidently. As Zig Ziglar used to say, "If everyone's throwing dirt—everyone's losing ground."

I have also observed that some people are just in love with their problems. I ask, "Is the drama in life more important than simply being happy and satisfied where you're at?" Wayne Dyer teaches, "Bloom where you're planted." Gratitude is the key, which offsets the temptation for envy as explained earlier in this book. It's important to lift others up with positivity rather than pull them down with negativity and then notice how others will love to be around you, rather than try to avoid you.

Along with my top three qualities, I have a list of twelve characteristics I look for in employees, which reflects a list of qualities I believe we should instill in our children (which I adapted from material presented by my friend and thought leader Richard Rossi at a Genius Network Mastermind event). When hiring, I want to find people who:

1. Are critical thinkers and problem-solvers
2. Conquer fear and build never-ending self-confidence
3. Can sell, persuade, and negotiate
4. Consistently set goals
5. Practice effective time-management
6. Actively listen, speak effectively, write articulately
7. Are likeable
8. Are entrepreneurial, innovative, and self-motivated
9. Practice consciously training the mind and body to unconsciously act in harmony with values and vision
10. Have the ability to take negative experiences in life and turn them into positive outcomes
11. Have an attitude of gratitude and an abundance mentality
12. Are always responsible and accountable

TAKING OWNERSHIP

It's also important to help employees take ownership in doing the right thing—whether that's solving a customer issue or coming up with a better resolution to a problem. A lot of times management might think they've empowered employees, but it gets lost in translation, leaving employees more focused on the letter of the law (out of fear), than on doing what's best.

For example, my wife and I wanted to get two deluxe swing sets, so the grandkids could enjoy them on family retreats and at Grandpa's Camp. I knew the president of a recreation equipment company, who had told me he'd be happy to give me a discount during the off-season. "Our sets are usually $3,000. I can give them to you for $1899—that's the same discount we'll be giving at the Home Show in the spring."

So one snowy day, Sharee and I stopped by one of their retail stores. We explained what the president had offered, and the clerk said, "That'll be $2,200 each, so $4,400." I tried again, articulating that the owner had told me he wanted to give me the Home Show price. The clerk said, "You ought to wait 'til the Home Show then."

I tried to appeal to common sense, asking, "Are things slow right now?" She replied, "Yes, we haven't sold anything for a while! But why don't you come back to the Home Show in two months, and you'll get the best deal?" I said, "I'm ready to take them today." She said, "Oh I wouldn't do that if I were you." I was flabbergasted.

While the $600 difference wasn't the end of the world, she was so inflexible, I ended up waiting until the Home and Garden Show to purchase the swing sets. Clearly she didn't feel she could take ownership in this situation—she was more worried about sticking to protocol.

Contrast that with companies like Nordstrom, whose employees are famously encouraged to do whatever it takes for the customer. I had a "Nordstrom" experience at our local Florsheim Shoes retailer several years ago.

I had just purchased a pair of shoes—well-appointed leather shoes with a beautiful sheen. I was wearing them on a Sunday drive, when Sharee and I were going up the canyon after church. As we were coming back down, Sharee said, "Stop! Do you see that bush?!" It was the first hint of fall, and the bush was a gorgeous fiery red. Sharee said, "I want those autumn leaves in my house. I want to do an arrangement!"

I looked at my clothes, my shoes, and the rocky ledge where that blazing bush was perched. I weighed my options, and chose the knight in shining armor path. As I headed out on the rocks to retrieve a few branches, I slipped and caught myself just in time. I was fine, but my brand new shoes were not. The finish came right off the top.

It was my fault walking in expensive dress shoes on a bunch of rocks, so I just thought, "Oh well, that was a waste of money, but I'm glad Sharee's got her red leaves."

I was in the mall not long after that, and I saw Bruce, my Florsheim salesman. He asked, "How are you enjoying those shoes?" I happened to be wearing them, and I said, "You won't believe what I did. I feel sick. They're all scraped up. I had them on when I went out on some rocks and slipped." He immediately said, "Oh, we'll replace them. Come right down here."

I hesitated, but he insisted, "Give me those shoes. I know it was your fault, but we stand behind our product. We don't want you walking around in Florsheim shoes that are scuffed up." I was blown away. And I also went back time and again for more Florsheim shoes.

You want to empower your employees to take negative experiences and turn them into positive outcomes. As they do, they'll feel a sense of contributing to the company, and help add to its abundance.

TEAM SPIRIT

Many companies offer "benefits" that require employees to get sick, quit or die to collect the perks. This focuses on scarcity, and I have to ask: what kind of benefits are those? In our company, we see it differently—we want our employees to enjoy the benefits of an abundant life in the workplace and in their personal lives. Part of that abundance comes through teamwork, because as I've said before, TEAM stands for Together Everyone Achieves More.

This is where holding Business Retreats with a Purpose can be valuable. Set aside a day or two—preferably away from the office—where you can blend a mix of fun with purposeful lessons on teamwork, abundance and empowerment. The time and resources invested can make a big difference as employees return to the tasks at the office with a renewed sense of abundance and cooperation.

With our staff, we have also instituted what we call Personal Development Days. Once a month, we meet outside the office at our cabin or somewhere special, and we focus on topics that can bring about personal growth. On one of our days, we discussed having a positive focus and aiming for three wins a day. During another, we explored how employees could develop KASH Blueprints and Legacy Banks with their own families. We've also covered how to deal with crises and deadlines, how to hold Family Retreats with a Purpose, and even how to buy real estate with little to no money down.

For one of our favorite company retreats, we did the Lunar Survival Exercise—one of many games and activities that we include in our Entitlement Abolition Kit. It was over the top as our entire team actually experienced why we get much better results when everyone is on board and giving their input. They all "got it" when the game proved in less than an hour that indeed, together we're better.

On another recent company retreat, I conducted our Conscious Communicator exercise, another of our Live Abundant tools. It only takes about forty-five minutes, and it dramatically improves communication between employees and supervisors, husbands and wives, business partners, company and customers/clients—really any relationship you care about. Following the exercise, communication always improves, and many of our employees shared that it was a game-changer when they went home and did it with their spouse and children. Whenever I do this exercise at couple retreats, I hear such comments between partners like, "No wonder you haven't understood me for twenty years!"

Recently, one of our great team members shared that he had received a handsome offer from another company to leave us and work for them. It would have been a sizable five-figure increase in salary. He said he turned it down without a second thought because the increase in salary would not make up for the non-monetary value he received by being part of our team. He explained he wanted to have a more abundant life, even more than he wanted a bigger paycheck. I was blown away and of course, have been even more appreciative of him for his loyalty and complement to our firm. You see, he's a tremendous asset—not a liability—like those people who just bide their time waiting for the next best offer. He and his sweet wife are very happy, because we're a Three-Dimensional firm.

EMPLOYEE ENGAGEMENT

In the pursuit of teamwork, it's also important to turn to employees for input on ways to improve the business, to help them feel part of the larger team, all working toward an end goal together.

One way to do this in your company is to hold regular employee feedback meetings. Organize them into teams (consider mixing people from different departments) who can tackle specific business problems. Ask for their candid, innovative insight.

But one word of caution: manage the size of the groups for this kind of open discussion. Be sure to keep the groups small enough to be productive—just big enough where you could feed them with two pizzas and two liters of beverage.

With groups this size, you start getting real, valuable feedback. Any larger, and you could be turning the room over to chaos—or just a couple strong personalities who dominate the discussion for everyone.

Another aspect of teamwork comes in how employees propel the company as a whole. Peter Drucker stated, "The business enterprise has two and only two basic functions; marketing and innovation. All the rest are costs." A lot of employees might think, "That's not my job. I'm not in marketing or R&D."

Walt Disney was one of those leaders who saw the value of turning to everyone on his team. One of Disneyland's most popular rides is Pirates of the Caribbean—even though it was created decades ago (it's one of my family's must-rides every time, too). When Walt Disney finished its construction, he had all of his employees experience it. At the end, he assembled all of them on the deck of the Blue Bayou Cafe to get their feedback. You see, one of the secrets to Walt Disney's success is that he invited input from others rather than relying solely on his own brilliance—he always made his cooperation greater than his status. In other words, he made every performance greater than the recognition or the applause that he would get (these are lifetime principles included in Dan Sullivan's book, *The Laws of Lifetime Growth*).

Two of the young girls that were in the kitchen did not think that he meant for them to come also. He asked where they were and the staff had to go retrieve them. When it was their turn to speak, they were asked what was missing on the ride. One of them said shyly, "Well

Mister Disney, where I come from, there are fireflies. I didn't see any fireflies." Disney said, "Brilliant!" and he called engineering and said, "We need to figure out how to make some fireflies." (How many of you enjoy those fireflies on that ride?)

Then the next young girl got courage and said, "Well Mister Disney, where I come from there are swamps. This does not smell like a swamp." Again, that was genius, so he got engineering to create the ambience and odors of a swamp. Disney understood that it was much better to cooperate than to simply think that he knew everything.

When I teach these principles to our team at work—everyone from our bookkeeper to our director of first impressions (our receptionist)—I explain I want them to do whatever they can to help the bigger picture. This means going beyond checking off their task lists every day; it means thinking through what they can do to help market the business, to innovate ways to help us grow. It can be in the way they talk about our company while at dinner with friends. It can be in noticing something like the travel issues we were having and finding ways to improve them.

Fredo Pareto, the Italian economist, taught increased productivity comes from continually identifying areas where you can achieve 80% of your results from 20% of your efforts. What I'm trying to do then, is give ownership to everybody in my company, encouraging them to come with ideas that can increase productivity with just 20% of their efforts, freeing them up to do other important things.

The French economist who coined the term entrepreneur, Jean-Baptiste Say, has said, "The entrepreneur shifts economic resources out of an area of lower and into an area of higher productivity and greater yield."

It's like Steve Jobs—he took what was already there, the MP3 player, and he made the iPod, putting a thousand songs in everybody's pocket. He didn't invent the cell phone, either, but he created a platform that has spawned over 1.2 million apps.

We've looked to bring our clients from lower productivity to higher productivity in all Three Dimensions of their Authentic Wealth, which has resulted in significant growth for our company over the years—and employees who take pride in their work, who enjoy working together as a team.

REWARD PERFORMANCE & MAKE IT FUN

Another way to avoid the "I want something for nothing" mentality is to establish a reward system that is clearly based on employee performance. Thomas S. Monson often shared the quote, "When performance is measured, performance improves. When performance is measured and reported, the rate of performance accelerates."

Identify the goals and behaviors you want to see in your company, make it transparent and attainable, and reinforce the positive behavior. Studies have shown rewards that matter to people are:

1. Monetary bonuses
2. Gifts or prizes
3. Prestige

We've rewarded employees with things like hotel suites for weekend stays with their spouses, cash bonuses, and gift cards. We recognize employees' breakthroughs and contributions in regular employee meetings. And we also have focused on making our environment fun.

We do things like summer barbecues for the employees and their families. We also host a day at Utah's largest theme park, Lagoon, where employees can enjoy the day with their families. Christmas dinners with white elephant gifts have become the highlight of the season every year. We also get involved in service projects, which enables employees to dedicate time to make a difference. All of this contributes to a sense of belonging, of feeling appreciated, and it has helped everyone stay abundance-minded.

SINCERELY INTERESTED

As company leaders, it's also important to be sincerely interested in your employees. Help them know that it's not just about you (or the company); it's also about their lives, their contribution, their talent. Listen to them. Understand them. Walk in their shoes. Develop a bond and uplift them, so they will feel better about their future or their situation after they interact with you.

Several years ago, there was a survey done with 1,000 surgeons. Out of all the surgeons, those doctors who spent at least sixteen minutes or more being sincerely interested in their patients—even if they made errors during surgery—were often forgiven by their patients. In other words, even in cases of grave mistakes, the chances of being sued were next to nil. Why? People felt their doctors cared, so they were more understanding in light of the errors.

The survey also revealed, however, that for every minute under sixteen that doctors did not invest being sincerely interested in their patients, their chances of being sued went up 10%. At that time, the HMOs were pushing for efficiency, urging their doctors to avoid wasting time with patients, encouraging them to see their work as a business where quantity of patients prevailed over quality of time invested. But they were being sued at higher rates and needed to discover why.

The survey showed that people don't tend to sue those they have relationships with. They sue doctors (and we can extend this to financial advisors, builders, or other professionals) whom they feel disconnected from. When things go wrong, patients don't have a relationship reservoir to offset the mistake. And often when they raise the complaint, to make matters worse, the disinterested professionals try to blame the client, or justify why they didn't accomplish the goal. Hence, all parties want to put the responsibility on circumstances or other people, but in the end if they had built a relationship, they would have been far better off.

The word *sincere* comes from ancient Italy (pronounced sin-chair-ay). There the potters would make pottery out of clay, and they would put it in a kiln or an oven. When it came out, it would often have cracks or imperfections. They learned that they could melt candle wax into the cracks, smooth them over, paint the pottery, and it would still be functional. It would hold water. But if it toppled over, where would it break? Yes, on the weak spots, right where the cracks lay hidden.

That's where the term "crackpot" comes from. Today we use crackpot to describe people who act like they have it all together, but when the first little bump comes along, they fall apart. They're not as strong as everybody thought they were.

Now going back to the Italian potters, if they produced a piece of pottery that did not have wax filler, they could label it "sincere," which means literally "without wax." So for us, being sincere means you're really the genuine, authentic person that people think you are. No wax fillers, paint, cover-ups, or hidden agendas. And being sincere is the key to true success with others. As you set the example for sincerity, that can extend to your employees and how they deal with each other, and with your customers.

THE MEANINGFUL TRANSFORMATION

In a book called *The Experience Economy,* the authors talk about the concept that generally people will pay more for something that, in their perception, provides a much greater value. This seems like a no-brainer, I know, but when the authors use the example of coffee in their book, it drives the point home. And it's a point that we can apply in our own lives.

They point out that coffee beans, at their pure commodity level, are probably worth about two cents a cup. When retailers take the beans, grind them and package the grounds to enable you to make a steaming hot cup at home, you are willing to pay twenty-five cents per cup or more for the unique product. Add convenience or exceptional service, and the value goes up even more—now maybe you're willing to pay a dollar or two at a place like a restaurant or a 7-Eleven.

But what happens when specialty shops take that basic commodity, turn it into a unique product, make it convenient, and then create a unique experience for you to enjoy that coffee? Yep, you're happily handing over $4 or $5.

When I travel to Chicago, I stop at a little Starbucks kiosk in the airport to get a poppy seed muffin or an orange juice. I'll wait ten or fifteen minutes in line, and I see people doing the same thing. They'll shell out $4 or $5 for an espresso-based cup of coffee, which is really just a few cents of liquid. Why are they doing that? It's because Starbucks has created its whole brand out of becoming that escape between the house and the office; they've created an ambiance with intriguing décor; they've added interesting music, an Internet café, and places for conversation. They've created value that people are willing to pay for, and they've become an international sensation for it.

It's not just coffee that folks will pay several times more than the base value for—it's all kinds of things ... even something as simple as water. I remember when a group of our friends took a motorcycle trip through Georgia and Florida. We shipped our Harley Davidsons down to Atlanta, rode down to Miami, and then our spouses flew in. We went down to Key West, came back through the Everglades, and ended up at the Disney theme parks for three days.

The first day at Disney World—one of the hottest May days on record—I stopped three times at a cart and shelled out $2.50 for a bottle of water. (This was back in 1999; those same bottles of water are now $4!) The crazy thing is we didn't bat an eye. We wanted the water, and we were willing to pay whatever Mickey was asking. At the end of the day, my last bottle was about half-full, and I chucked it in the trash without thinking a thing of it.

Then we went out and filled up our Harley Davidsons with premium gasoline at $1.60 a gallon. Remember this was 1999, so at the time we screamed highway robbery because back in Utah, premium was only $1.30 a gallon.

Now do the math. How many ounces in a gallon? There are 128. We were paying the equivalent of $16 a gallon for water and throwing it in the trash. But we were outraged at paying $1.60 a gallon for gas. See how transforming a basic commodity into a unique product, adding convenience, and creating a unique experience around it can add incredible value that people are willing to pay for?

How can we apply this at work, in the community, and at home? With your business, when you find ways to take what you offer, make it truly unique, add convenience, and/or create a unique experience, your customers will be willing to pay a premium for it. In the community, when you help a cause, your church, or a charity by adding your unique talents or means, you're elevating their efforts. And at home, when you share your knowledge, skills, insight, and wisdom with children and grandchildren, you've passed along your unique value. Taking it a step further, if you can help people experience a meaningful transformation—something that changes their quality of life, their relationships, their financial outlook, or whatever it is that is deeply meaningful—you've now taken it to an all new level.

This is what people will grant the highest value. You'll have the highest compensation with the least competition. You'll create loyalty, or what we call a value-creation monopoly. They'll come to you because you're the catalyst for their meaningful transformation. They want that purpose and change, that abundant life you're helping provide. And in turn, you'll have the satisfaction of propelling others, which will come back to you in all kinds of abundance.

With these tools and perspectives in place, you *can* tackle entitlement in the workplace. Remember to do it one step at a time. It doesn't have to happen overnight. As you begin to focus on things like encouraging ingenuity, hiring the right people, and rewarding performance, you will open the way for a transformation that can bring about greater overall abundance. As my friend Dan Sullivan puts it, "Choose to be in the *transformational* business, or you will forever be trapped in the *transactional* business."

chapter 12

Determine the Life You'll Lead and the Legacy You'll Leave

" Carve your name on hearts, not tombstones.
A legacy is etched into the minds of others
and the stories they share about you."

Shannon L. Alder

As I've mentioned, a few times a year, my team and I present multi-day events that help families learn many of the same principles you're exploring in this book. At our Abundance by Choice events, we often ask our audiences to consider two simple but far-reaching questions:

What kind of LIFE do you want to LEAD?

What kind of LEGACY do you want to LEAVE?

Really, that's what it all comes down to. Every day we make countless choices that add up to the sum of who we are, the kind of life we're leading, and the kind of legacy we're leaving.

Too many people live on autopilot, slogging through the day-to-day duties (mostly focused on earning money or maintaining the family schedule), eating a meal or two, watching a show or two, clicking on an article or two, falling asleep, then waking up to do it all over again.

This is zombie living, or unconscious living. But what if instead, as noted in Chapter 6, we followed William George Jordan's advice to consciously train the mind and body to unconsciously act in harmony with our values and vision? This of course requires us to define our values and vision, and then take steps to incorporate them ... but just think about the results. It could be transformative, not just for yourself, but for your posterity.

So now, let's think about the knowledge and perspective you've gained throughout your journey with this book—the kind of stuff that can help you shape that all-important values and vision. You've learned how to:

- Identify the difference between entitlement and empowerment

- Discover how to leave the Scarcity Cycle behind and thrive in the Abundance Cycle

- Determine where your family exists on the Entitlement vs. Abundance Spectrum

- Understand the Three Dimensions of Authentic Wealth

- Establish your own Legacy Bank and KASH Blueprint to ensure generational wealth in the Legacy Dimensions (Foundational and Intellectual)

- Capture and reinforce your Legacy Dimensions by holding regular gatherings like Family and Business Retreats with a Purpose and Grandpa's Camp

- Explore financial vehicles that will help you optimize your Financial Dimension for generations to come

Hopefully you're feeling energized about the possibilities that you can now see for your family or business; you've gained clarity on where you are and where you want to go; and you have the essential road-map and strategies to get there.

But you also might be feeling like, "What's next? And how do I possibly maintain this momentum?"

If so, feeling this way is completely normal.

I've been teaching Live Abundant strategies in national presentations, large group seminars, corporate events, smaller group retreats, and one-on-one client sessions for decades. In all that time, I've seen some common patterns.

There is the initial inspired willingness to learn, followed by the mo-tivated desire to make true changes. This euphoric period of clarity and excitement can last a few days or even weeks ... but then it often meets up with one or more of what I call Resistance Rascals. You may have encountered them before—they include:

a. Foggy perspectives from the past that cloud your new vision

b. Timeworn ruts with a gravitational force strong enough to pull you back into old behaviors

c. Pushback from loved ones who aren't familiar with your brighter path

d. The maybe-I-should-give-up fatigue that comes from realiz-ing how long true transformation can take

e. All of the above

Did you relate to "e. All of the above"? If so, you're in good company. This is just the reality of change. It isn't easy. But just because it's not a cake walk doesn't mean you shouldn't have your cake and eat it too. Abundance simply takes effort, and reinforcement.

CULTURAL SHIFT

My family and I like to spend time in the outdoors, and our home state of Utah is the perfect place to support our adventures. We enjoy time at our cabin, where it's not uncommon to see deer and elk right outside our front window. I have a Jeep Rubicon that can just about climb a tree, and believe me, we've done everything short of that in places like Moab, Hell's Chute, and Cyclone Pass in the Wind Rivers range. We also like to go fishing—my grandkids are still trying to out-fish Grandpa, but so far I'm holding strong on the title. And we like to hike. We've spent many unforgettable hours in national parks like Zion and Bryce Canyon.

In any part of nature—especially the awe-inspiring parks—one thing becomes clear. Change is most often gradual. As you stand at the base of those sandstone and limestone monoliths, you see the effect of water, wind, and the earth's upheaval carving, shaping, and sculpting the rock over countless generations.

I think our lives are like that. The kind of change we seek doesn't happen overnight. It is the result of earnest, consistent effort that becomes habit. These habits slowly smooth our rough edges and leave us more inspired—and inspiring—than when we began.

As you look at your personal journey toward greater abundance, and the one you want to help take your family on, it might help to relax a little, take a breath, and realize it will not be a universal change in just a few weeks, or even months. And that is okay—that is as it should be.

When you're embarking on changing big things, you're essentially setting out to transform the entire culture of your family. It can start as a ripple in a pond—drop that first stone and watch the effect emanate all the way to the shore. Everything you do, even the tiniest first actions, can have an impact on your family. It is okay to recognize that your family's shift will likely be gradual.

The important thing to do is to take that first step, to decide that you want to make these changes. It's interesting how many people choose not to make decisions. They have "decidephobia." But while they hem and haw, what they don't realize is they're putting off a brighter future. When we make a decision we are free to move forward, but when we avoid deciding, we often dwell in the past, or worse, keep repeating patterns expecting different results. Often when we find people not willing to decide, they experience chaos in their lives.

I think it's interesting to note the word decide comes from the root word "cide," which actually means to kill off. (Homicide is the act of killing another human being. Suicide is the act of killing oneself. Pesticide is the act of killing pests.) When you decide, you're killing off the alternatives and taking steps toward (hopefully) a better path.

"Choose" is a future-based word. We teach our children and grandchildren to decide to live a life of abundance versus scarcity, to always look forward to a happier future, rather than trying to change the past. Yes, we want to learn from our experiences, but we want to decide which part of the past gets to come along for the ride, and we leave the rest behind.

When I decided to marry Sharee over forty years ago, basically, I "killed off" all other alternatives of thinking or considering other women in a romantic, intimate way. I think this is one of the reasons why we have been so happily married for more than forty years.

Just the same, as you decide to make changes with your family, you're essentially "killing off" the patterns of the past, and taking those first steps toward leading your family toward a brighter, more abundant future.

This process of change can happen with more than just families—it can happen in the workplace, and even within communities. I saw it in action when Sharee and I joined my brother-in-law, Dr. Roy Hammond, and my sister Glenda on one of their humanitarian trips to the Dominican Republic.

Roy and Glenda's charitable organization, Smiles for Hope, had partnered with Esperanza, a nonprofit there dedicated to helping people improve their lives through microloan programs. We had the opportunity to meet with people, mostly women, who had started their own businesses through this program. One woman shared that with her first microloan, she had opened a hair salon.

It was very simple: a shade tarp and basic hair styling equipment. She had made enough to pay off the loan and acquire another loan, and another, until she eventually grew her business so large that she owned a strip mall. She had also gone on to build a school and was mentoring other women through the business development process. With that initial small loan of $200, she had made the decision to improve her life, and eventually ended up improving the lives of countless members of her community.

As of 2013, Esperanza had loaned out in excess of $38 million in microloans averaging about $200, with a remarkable 97.5% pay-back rate! It's amazing that when we give people a hand up instead of a handout, responsibility and accountability increase, and significant results can follow.

MAKING THE SHIFT ... IN STAGES

As you move forward, think of creating your family's change in stages. For example, if your children are accustomed to you paying for things like cars or school tuition, it will come as a shock to learn they will now be required to put some skin in the game and help pay for at least part of the expense—or pay you back at a nominal interest rate if they don't have the means now.

Rather than just announcing and enforcing the change, you will likely want to start shifting the thinking in the family first. You can begin by sharing the concepts of responsibility and accountability. At another gathering, you can relay the story of the caterpillars and the chrysalis.

Later, you can let the family know because you love them, you want to help them become their best selves, which means taking more owner-ship in the responsibility of life—you might want to have fun with it by using the $2 Rule.

Once these concepts become part of the family conversation, then you can explain you're going to start applying that principle of respon-sibility and accountability to some of the practical things of life, like buying a car, or paying for school.

You may want to involve your children in developing the plan—is it an expense you'll divide, say 70% and 30%, or will they borrow money and pay you back at 1% to 3% interest? Determine things like a time-line for payment, and a back-up plan if they aren't able to cover their portion of the cost. For example, if they can't meet the loan payments for a car, they can trade the value of those payments by doing repair work or landscaping around your house until they are in position to pay again.

To help you get an idea of what I'm talking about, let me share a sto-ry about my daughter Mindy and her husband Brian. Brian had just graduated from Brigham Young University, and they had a ninety-day window before they would leave for Iowa to attend dental school.

They were trying to find ways to get through the next few years with as little student loan debt as possible. Mindy had been doing some research. She worked at a spa in Utah and saw that estheticians made great money and enjoyed flexibility in their schedule. She contacted a high-end spa in Iowa City and found out they didn't have an estheti-cian. She decided that if she could get her license before they moved, she would be qualified to take that position, earning a percentage per treatment and tips that would be at least three times what other young people make in a college town.

She filled out a Solution Formulator (one of the tools in our tool belt that we originally adapted from my good friend Strategic Coach Dan Sullivan) and presented it to Sharee and me. Her plan: during this ninety-day window that she and Brian had before moving to Iowa, she proposed that they move down to St. George and stay in our family condo. She could attend esthetician school there, and in exchange for rent, she and Brian could handle the repairs we'd been meaning to get to, paint the rooms, etc.

She explained with all their planning, they would still be $2,000 short. She asked to borrow that amount, and based on her projected income, she could pay us back over a certain amount of time. She also explained the bonus benefits of her plan—she would work at the spa in Iowa City for a year, gaining a clientele and valuable experience (including confidence and increased social skills) to help her when she and Brian hoped to start a family during their second year.

It was solid thinking, so we were on board. And sure enough, it all played out according to her plan. But the key was, she made a plan and worked the plan, with adjustments along the way. Mindy's career as an esthetician provided a comfortable dental school life, and empowered them to start their family. In addition to her cosmetology skills, she also transitioned to becoming an incredible client relationship manager with our firm, working from home while mothering their little daughters.

You see, when you're in motion, creating transformations, this processional added value creates "strategic by-products." Dan Sullivan says, "Strategic By-Products take the form of new knowledge, opportunities, and innovations which take us in the realm of surprises that break us away from our original way of thinking that ultimately can lead us to a far superior result than what we were initially aiming for."

Now I share this as an example of how this whole concept of responsibility and accountability, as well as the family's Legacy Bank and KASH Blueprint, can be a working, functioning part of the fabric of your family's life, empowering your children to move forward in positive ways.

Your family's patterns and strategies may not be there yet, but you *can* get there. Just plan to make that shift in stages, rethink your family's thinking, and redirect the way your family works as a team to achieve success.

If it feels like you may have an uphill battle ahead, don't get discouraged, and above all, don't fall into the pit of guilt—a quagmire I've seen too many families get stuck in. The very fact that you're reading this book shows that you are a forward-thinking parent who wants to do what's best for your family. It shows you want to be a leader, which doesn't mean you have to be an expert. My son can go on a trail once or twice and be ready to lead the rest of us on it, even if he doesn't know every flora and fauna, every rock and dip along the way. Take heart in your own opportunity to lead and learn as you go, and move forward one step at a time.

I've often heard from those who attend our Abundance by Choice events that they love everything they've learned, but it can sometimes feel like drinking from a firehose. There's a lot of information; it's true!

The concepts we share are essentially the best of the best out there in terms of abundant living. It's all been gleaned from the thirty-plus years I've been involved in some of the nation's top think tanks and professional organizations. It's the culmination of the $3 million-plus I've invested personally to be a part of exclusive groups of forward thinkers. And it's the optimal learning our Wealth Architects and partners have contributed from their professional and personal experience, as well.

Essentially, the Live Abundant team is a collection of people dedicated to the highest ideals of living, people who are working to implement these same principles in our own families, who are committed to sharing these concepts with our clients.

It's been thrilling to see the progress our clients have made in their own lives, and it's exciting to see us taking the learning to the next level with our latest focus: the Entitlement Abolition Kit *(see www. EntilementAbolition.com).*

THE POWER OF COACHING

As anyone who has played or watched sports knows, there's not an athlete on the planet who has improved his or her game without a coach.

In boxing, the world's most prized fighters can train every day, hours a day, to face an opponent just once a year. Olympians work with the globe's best coaches through grueling daily sessions just for that chance at gold every four years.

Professional teams hire specialized coaches for virtually every aspect of the game. Look at Major League Baseball, for example. Each team boasts a roster of experts to help their players win, which can include:

- Bench Coach
- 1st Base Coach
- 3rd Base Coach
- Hitting Coach
- Assistant Hitting Coach
- Pitching Coach
- Bullpen Coach
- Strength & Conditioning Coach

The top players often take it to another level in the off-season, enlisting the services of high-end coaching programs that use technology and analytics to review every aspect of their game, stance, swing, and agility, and make adjustments that can help edge out the competition.

Look at our own lives. If you've had kids, you've likely driven them more than a few times to practice for soccer, baseball, football, lacrosse, ballet, tap, jazz, hip hop, guitar, piano, painting ... and the list can go on and on.

In our culture we certainly appreciate the value of coaching in everything from sports to the arts. Why then, is it somewhat novel, to apply that same advantage to the areas of our lives that perhaps matter most—our family dynamics and patterns, our intellectual and foundational assets ... our abundance? Inspiration leads to motivation, but we often need help taking that final step: implementation. I hate to think where I would be if I didn't have coaches.

This is why we've developed the Entitlement Abolition Kit. Families were hungry for guidance and reinforcement in making the cultural shift necessary to open the way for abundant living. They wanted help incorporating the habits of abundance, the tools for successful living, like The Better Life Circle and The Appreciation Accelerator. They wanted someone to turn to when the going got a little tough, and the kids were putting up resistance. They wanted insight on developing their family's values and vision, as well as the KASH Blueprint.

The Entitlement Abolition Kit serves as a "virtual, digital Legacy Coach," a do-it-yourself guide to incorporating these principles. Because we believe there are four primary ways to combat entitlement, each of the four kit modules focuses on these four areas of transformation:

Module 1: Habits of Abundance
- Shift from scarcity to abundance
- Improve your relationships in just 30 days
- Teach accountability and responsibility
- Conquer first-world problems
- Develop a Values & Vision Statement

Module 2: Developing Your KASH Blueprint
- Develop your own family rules of governance
- Why Equal Opportunity Trusts are more powerful than equal distribution
- How to avoid the mistakes that plague generational wealth
- Powerful keys to unifying your family through values and vision

Module 3: Family Retreats with a Purpose
- Plan and hold your first Family Retreat with a Purpose
- Unite your family through purpose driven adventures
- Create a family culture of growth, wealth, and possibility
- Gain in-depth access to sample agendas and itineraries

Module 4: Building Your Legacy Bank
- How to make deposits into your Legacy Bank
- Capturing your family KASH
- How to conduct and record a powerful life sketch
- Pass your swing (not just the clubs) to future generations

The kit's guidance has already proven invaluable for participants, as it provides a realistic framework for implementing that gradual shift and incorporating abundance tools and strategies. Our Legacy Coaches are dedicated experts who understand the foundations of human psychology, the principles of sequential learning, and who themselves are parents, living the day-to-day realities of raising families with abundant living principles.

GET IN MOTION

Whether you enlist the support of the Entitlement Abolition Kit, or you develop your own plan for abolishing entitlement and increasing abundance in your family, my greatest hope for you is that you simply: Get. In. Motion.

Think of entitlement as a tree. You don't want to just lop off a few branches here and there. You want to get to the root of the problem. An arborist knows that the roots extend just as far as the branches, so make sure to get all the way to the core of what's holding your family back from abundance. As you do, change can start to really take place.

Keep in mind, you don't have to approach everything exactly the way I do. There are at least a hundred different ways these principles can be applied. Every person we teach implements these strategies in different ways—it looks a little different for every family as they apply what works best for them.

Perhaps your Family Retreats with a Purpose will have a more flexible agenda—one that simply includes fifteen minutes of learning in the morning and evening. Maybe your Grandpa's Camp will be an afternoon in your backyard every summer. Maybe your family's Values & Vision Statement will be just one sentence long. Your approach can be as structured or as relaxed as you need. Remember, your strategies for entitlement-free, abundant living should correspond with your family's personality and work for you. In the end, it's all about loving the people in your life and lifting them up to see a vision of a brighter future.

And keep in mind, you don't have to do it all at once. Identify even just one or two strategies from this book that you want to implement, collaborate with your spouse, involve your family, put one foot in front of the other, and begin today to get on the road to a brighter future.

This reminds me of a favorite story I share in *Learning Curves,* a book filled with more than ninety short drop-in-your-lap lessons you can share with your family. This particular story is that of Homan J. Walsh. When Homan died in Lincoln, Nebraska, on March 8, 1899, local newspapers noted that he had been a thirty-year resident of the city, a real estate businessman, an officer of the Lincoln Gas Company, and a past city council member. Of greater interest to Nebraskans, both then and now, was Walsh's unique boyhood contribution to the building of the first suspension bridge over the Niagara River. The *Nebraska State Journal,* as well as other newspapers around the country, used the occasion of his death to recall the unusual story for readers.

In 1848 Walsh, then a boy in New York state, played a key role in the construction of the first suspension bridge across the Niagara River between the United States and Canada. In the fall of 1847, civil engineer Charles Ellet, Jr. of Philadelphia was commissioned to construct such a bridge at the narrowest point of the Niagara gorge, immediately above the Whirlpool Rapids. Ellet was about to begin when he faced his first obstacle. The building of a suspension bridge is begun with the stretching of a line or wire across the stream. However, the turbulent rapids, the 800-foot-wide gap, and the 225-foot-high cliffs of the Whirlpool Gorge made a direct crossing impossible.

It occurred to someone that a kite might be a way to bridge the chasm. Accordingly, a cash prize was offered to the first boy who could fly his kite, with a line attached, to the opposite bank. There was a tremendous turnout of American and Canadian boys for a contest held in January 1848. The first to succeed in spanning the gorge with his kite, named the Union, was a young American, Homan J. Walsh.

In order to take advantage of more favorable winds, Walsh crossed to the Canadian side of the gorge by ferry just below Niagara Falls, and walked the two miles along the top of the cliff to the bridge site. At midnight, when a lull in the wind occurred, he flew his kite high above the gorge, and it reached the American side. Then there was a sudden pull of the line, and it went limp. It had broken. To make matters worse, Walsh found himself marooned in Canada for eight days because river ice prevented the ferry from operating.

Finally, Walsh was able to cross to the American side of the river and retrieve his kite. He then returned to the Canadian side, where he again flew the kite to the opposite bank. The kite string was fastened to a tree on the American shoreline, and a cord attached to it was pulled across. This time it didn't break. Next came a heavier cord, then a rope, and finally a wire cable, which was the beginning of the new bridge, completed on July 26, 1848.

Sometimes, the building of a strong bridge between generations starts with a small string and persistence as the ties become stronger and stronger.

However you approach it, however you decide to start building your generational bridge, just get going. Because I can tell you, the rewards are sweet. As Sharee and I look at our six children and fourteen grandchildren, there is no greater joy than knowing they have the tools and foundations for lives of responsibility, accountability, and abundance. They have not only inherited KASH from Sharee and me, but they are accumulating their own. As an extended family, we are gathering all of that KASH in our Legacy Bank, so it can be passed down to future generations.

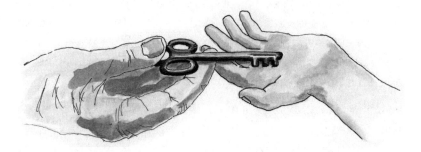

Does that mean the Andrew family's lives are perfect? Definitely not. Do we still struggle and face challenges? Of course. But we are there for each other. And we have the tools to continue to learn from life's difficulties, make adjustments, and press on. I can tell you, if you work it … it works.

I wish you and your family all the best as you look to abolish entitlement and thrive in abundance. And may you find joy in leading your family, and leaving a legacy.

www.EntitlementAbolition.com